GOD RESCUES HIS PEOPLE

THE STORY BIBLE SERIES

1. *God's Family* tells the story of creation, God's promises to Abraham's family, and the adventures of Joseph.

2. *God Rescues His People* tells about Israel's escape from Egypt, Moses and the Ten Commandments, and the wandering in the wilderness.

3. *God Gives the Land* tells the story of Joshua, the adventures of the judges, and the story of Ruth.

4. *God's Chosen King* tells about Samuel, Saul, and David, God's promises to David's family, and the Psalms.

5. *God's Wisdom and Power* tells about the glorious reign of Solomon, the wonderful works of Elijah and Elisha, and the Proverbs and the Song of Songs.

6. *God's Justice* tells the story of the prophets Amos, Hosea, Isaiah, and Jeremiah and their messages of God's judgment and mercy.

7. *God Comforts His People* tells about God's people in exile, their return to Judah, and the adventures of Esther and Daniel.

8. *God Sends His Son* tells about God sending Jesus to set up his kingdom.

9. *God's Suffering Servant* tells about the last week of Jesus' life, his suffering, death, and resurrection.

10. *God Builds His Church* tells about the coming of the Holy Spirit, the adventures of the apostles, and John's vision of the end of the world.

Story Bible Series, Book 2

GOD RESCUES HIS PEOPLE

Stories of God and His People from Exodus, Leviticus, Numbers, and Deuteronomy

Retold by Eve B. MacMaster
Illustrated by James Converse

HERALD PRESS
Scottdale, Pennsylvania
Waterloo, Ontario

Library of Congress Cataloging in Publication Data

MacMaster, Eve, 1942-
　God rescues his people.

　(story Bible series; bk. 2)
　1. Moses (Biblical leader)—Juvenile literature.
2. Bible stories, English—O.T.　Pentateuch.　I. Title.
II. Series.
BS580.M6M28　　　222'.109505　　　82-2849
ISBN 0-8361-1994-0 (pbk.)　　　AACR2

The paper used in this publication is recycled and meets
the minimum requirements of American National
Standard for Information Sciences—Permanence of Paper
for Printed Library Materials, ANSI Z39.48-1984.

GOD RESCUES HIS PEOPLE
Copyright © 1982 by Herald Press, Scottdale, Pa. 15683
　Published simultaneously in Canada by Herald Press,
　Waterloo, Ont. N2L 6H7. All rights reserved
Library of Congress Catalog Card Number: 82-2849
International Standard Book Number: 0-8361-1994-0
Printed in the United States of America
Design: Alice B. Shetler

99 98 97 96 95 94 93 10 9 8 7 6 5 4 3 2

Author's Note

God Rescues His People is Book 2 of the Herald Press Story Bible Series. This series retells the complete story of God and his people as recorded in the Bible.

These stories were first written down centuries ago in the Hebrew language to tell about God's actions in human history. They have been translated and retold many times, because people everywhere want to know what God is like.

The Bible tells us that God is a person. As we read about him and his relationships with the people in the Bible, we discover his personality.

The first book of the Story Bible Series, *God's Family*, tells how God made the world and people and how he chose one family from all the families on earth to begin his work of salvation.

This second book tells how God's family becomes the nation of Israel, a small nation with a great God. Moses, the servant of God, leads God's people out of slavery in Egypt, teaches them God's law at Mount Sinai, and brings them through the great and terrible wilderness to the very edge of the Promised Land.

It is my hope that readers of all faiths, young and old, will experience as much joy and excitement in reading these stories as I have had in telling them.

Many of God's people have given their time, advice, and

encouragement, making this truly a shared labor of love. My advisory committee, who read the manuscript in its early stages, includes Bible professors George R. Brunk III, Ronald D. Guengerich, G. Irvin Lehman, and Kenneth Seitz; childhood curriculum and librarian specialists Elsie E. Lehman and A. Arlene Bumbaugh; and Choice Books executive Angie B. Williams. My editor, Paul M. Schrock of Herald Press, has been patient and helpful at every stage.

My family have shared their lives with the book. Sam, Tom, and Sarah MacMaster have carefully tested each story. Richard MacMaster has been an unfailing source of support.

To them and to everyone else who has helped with words of encouragement, this book is dedicated.

Eve MacMaster
Bridgewater, Virginia
Advent, 1981

Contents

God Rescues His People
1. Slaves in Egypt — 11
2. A Princess Rescues a Baby — 17
3. Moses Tries to Save His People — 21
4. The Voice from the Burning Bush — 25
5. "Let My People Go!" — 30
6. God Strikes the Egyptians — 35
7. The Blood of the Lamb — 44
8. Crossing the Sea — 49

God Makes an Agreement with His People
9. Bread from Heaven — 57
10. Water from a Rock — 63
11. The Ten Commandments — 67
12. An Agreement Signed in Blood — 72
13. The Story of the Golden Calf — 76
14. God Gives the People Another Chance — 81
15. God's Tabernacle in the Wilderness — 86
16. Worshiping the Lord — 93
17. Unholy Fire! — 99
18. The Goat That Was Sent Away — 103
19. A Calendar for God's People — 107

God Teaches His People
   20. Marching Orders — 113
   21. The Graves of Greed — 118
   22. The Spies Who Were Afraid of Giants — 124
   23. Angry Rebels and Aaron's Rod — 131
   24. Moses Disobeys God — 137
   25. God Fights the Canaanite Kings — 142
   26. Balaam and His Blessings — 146
   27. Don't Worship Idols! — 155
   28. Remembering God's Teaching — 160
   29. Choose Life! — 164

Map: The World of Moses — 56

The Author — 168

God Rescues
His People

Slaves in Egypt

Exodus 1

THE king of the Egyptians was the greatest king in the world, and his people were the greatest nation. Egypt was a rich, fertile land that stretched like a green ribbon through the dry, sandy desert. The rich black soil of Egypt was well-watered by the mighty river Nile.

In ancient times the Egyptians built great cities and canals and stone monuments beside the Nile, and they made enormous tombs, called pyramids, where they buried their kings. The Egyptians worshiped many gods, including the

Nile and the sun and their king, who was called Pharaoh. Their greatest god was the god of the dead.

The Egyptian army kept enemies out of their country with the power of horse-drawn chariots and well-trained soldiers. The horses and their riders struck fear into the hearts of the people of other nations. Everyone was afraid of Egypt.

No one was afraid of Israel. The Israelites were one of the smallest nations in the world. They were poor shepherds who owned no land and commanded no army. They worshiped the living God, the creator of heaven and earth. But who on earth had ever heard of the Israelites or their God?

When they first came to Egypt, the Israelites were a family of seventy people. They came because they were hungry. It was a time of great famine, and they could find little to eat or drink where they lived, in the land of Canaan.

The father of the family was Jacob, who was also called Israel. He arrived with his eleven sons and their wives and children. Another son, Joseph, was already living in Egypt. Joseph helped the family find a place to live in a part of Egypt named Goshen. The green fields of Goshen were the best in the land. Since Joseph had helped the Egyptians during the famine, they were glad to make room for his family.

Before he died, Joseph told his brothers, "God will remember you and take you back to Canaan, for he promised that land to Jacob and to Jacob's father, Isaac, and to Isaac's father, Abraham. He told them they would become a great nation and he would give them the land. So when God brings you out of Egypt, be sure to take my bones with you."

After Joseph's death, his brothers wrapped his body like a mummy, so it wouldn't decay, and put it in a stone coffin above the ground. As the years passed, the parents told the children about Joseph and why his coffin wasn't buried and about God's promise to Abraham, Isaac, and Jacob.

The children and grandchildren of Jacob and those who came after them—their descendants—grew into a large nation, so many that they soon filled the land of Goshen.

The nation of Jacob's descendants was made up of tribes, family groups named for each of Jacob's sons: Reuben, Simeon, Levi, Judah, Issachar, Zebulun, Benjamin, Dan, Naphtali, Gad, and Asher, plus the tribes of Joseph's sons, Manasseh and Ephraim.

The Egyptians called them Hebrews, because they were wandering people without land of their own. They called themselves the children of Israel, or Israelites.

At first the Egyptians were kind to the Israelites, because they remembered Joseph. For many years the Israelites lived comfortably in Goshen, tending their flocks and fields.

Then a new king, who had never heard of Joseph, came to the throne of Egypt. This king, called "Pharaoh" (like all Egyptian kings), noticed how the Israelites were filling up the land.

"Let's do something about these Hebrews!" he said to his people. "There are so many of them, they're dangerous! What if there's a war? They might join our enemies and fight against us!"

So the Egyptians made the Israelites go to work for them. They forced them to build Pharaoh's storage cities, Pithom and Rameses, where they kept grain and weapons for the army.

In spite of this bad treatment, the Israelites kept on growing. It seemed that the worse the Egyptians treated them, the more they spread out. After a while the Egyptians could hardly stand the sight of them.

Next they made slaves of the Israelites, forcing them to do all sorts of field work and brick-making for their building projects. The Israelites were miserable, but the Egyptians felt no pity for them.

And still the Israelites kept increasing in number.

Then Pharaoh called in Shiphrah and Puah, two Israelite midwives who helped their people when babies were born.

He told them, "When you go to their homes to help the Hebrew women have their babies, watch carefully. If the baby is a girl, let her live. But if it is a boy, kill him!"

The midwives knew that God wouldn't want them to kill the babies, so they disobeyed the king.

When Pharaoh heard about this, he sent for them.

"What are you doing?" he demanded. "Why are you letting the boy babies live?"

"Hebrew mothers aren't like Egyptian women," Shiphrah and Puah answered. "They're strong, and their babies are usually already born when we get there."

Although the king was angry with the midwives, God was pleased with them. He rewarded

them by giving them homes and families of their own.

Meanwhile, the Israelites were still increasing. Pharaoh had another idea.

"Take every newborn Hebrew boy and throw it into the Nile!" he ordered his people.

A Princess Rescues a Baby

Exodus 2

"THE Egyptians are killing our babies!"
"Hide them!"
"Save them!"
"Do something!"

The Israelites tried everything to keep the Egyptians from throwing their baby boys into the Nile. One husband and wife, Amran and Jochabed, already had a daughter named Miriam and a three-year-old son named Aaron when a beautiful baby boy was born to them. They hid the baby from the Egyptians for three months,

and then Jochabed thought of on a plan to save him.

She took a box made of reeds, like a basket, covered it with clay and tar to make it waterproof, and laid her baby in it. Then she placed the little floating cradle in the high grass along the banks of the Nile. She told Miriam to stay near the river to see what would happen to her baby brother.

After a while Pharaoh's daughter came down to the river to bathe. While her maids walked along the bank, the princess went into the water. There she saw the reed box floating like a little boat among the tall grasses. She sent one of the maids to get it.

What was in the box?

The princess took it from her maid and opened it herself. Inside was a little baby boy, and he was crying!

She felt pity for the baby. "Look!" she said, "it's one of the Hebrew babies!"

Just then Miriam came up to her. "Shall I go find a Hebrew woman to nurse the baby?" she asked.

"Yes, Go!" answered the princess.

In a few minutes Miriam returned with Jochabed.

"Take this baby and nurse him for me," the princess said, "and I'll pay you."

So Jochabed took her baby home and nursed him. She knew that nobody could harm him now, for he was under the protection of Pharaoh's daughter!

When the child was old enough to leave his mother, Jochabed brought him to the palace. The princess was delighted with him. She adopted the boy and named him Moses (which means "pulled out" or "saved"). "I pulled him out of the water," the princess said, hugging him.

Moses grew up in Pharaoh's family, the adopted son of Pharaoh's daughter. He lived in a palace and dressed in fine clothes. He learned Egyptian writing, Egyptian law, and Egyptian customs, but in his heart he knew that the Israelites were his people.

3

Moses Tries to Save His People

Exodus 2

ONE day after Moses had grown up, he went out from the palace to visit his people. While he was living a comfortable life as an Egyptian prince, the Israelites were working as slaves, and Moses wanted to help them.

During his visit Moses saw an Egyptian hit an Israelite. He felt he had to do something.

He looked all around. Nobody was watching.

Moses struck the Egyptian and killed him. Then he hid the body in the sand.

The next day he went back to the same place.

This time he saw two Israelites fighting with each other, and again he wanted to help.

"Why are you beating up one of your own people?" he asked the one who was in the wrong.

The man pushed him aside. "Who made you our ruler and judge?" he asked. "Are you going to kill me as you killed that Egyptian yesterday?"

Moses felt afraid. "They've found out what I've done!" he said to himself.

The story of the murder spread until Pharaoh heard about it and ordered his men to kill Moses.

Moses ran away. He left Egypt and went out to the land of Midian in the southeastern desert, far from the power of Pharaoh and his men.

While Moses was resting by a well, he saw seven young women come to draw water for their sheep and goats. He watched them pull their buckets up from the well and fill the troughs for their animals. But before their animals could drink, some shepherds came and drove the women away and took the water for their own animals.

Moses wanted to do something to help, so he got up and refilled the troughs.

The young women went home to their father, a priest of Midian named Jethro.

"Why are you home so early today?" he asked them.

"An Egyptian rescued us from the shepherds," they answered. "He even drew water for us and gave it to our animals."

"Well, then, where is he? Why did you leave him out there in the wilderness? Go and invite him to eat with us!"

Moses accepted their invitation and stayed with Jethro and his family. They became good friends. After a while Moses married Zipporah, one of Jethro's daughters.

Moses and Zipporah had two sons. Moses named the first one Gershom (meaning "sojourner") "because," he said, "I'm a sojourner, a foreigner living in this land."

Later, when their second son was born, Moses said, "God has been my helper. He has saved me from Pharaoh's sword," and he named the child

Eliezer, meaning "God is my helper."

Now, instead of fine Egyptian linen, Moses wore rough wool clothing, and instead of a palace, he lived in a simple hut. Instead of sitting on a beautifully painted chair and eating a rich feast at a table, he sat on the ground and ate a simple shepherd's meal. He took off his jewelry and let his beard grow. No one in Egypt would recognize him now.

Moses spent forty years taking care of his father-in-law's sheep and goats and learning his way among the rocks and hills and watering places in the wilderness. He thought he would never see Egypt or the Israelites again.

Then, finally, the king of Egypt and all those who had tried to kill Moses died.

But the new king treated the Israelites even more cruelly. They groaned and cried out in their slavery, "Save us from this misery! Help us! Rescue us!"

Their cries rose up to God, who saw their suffering and felt pity for them. He was ready to keep his promise. He was ready to rescue his people.

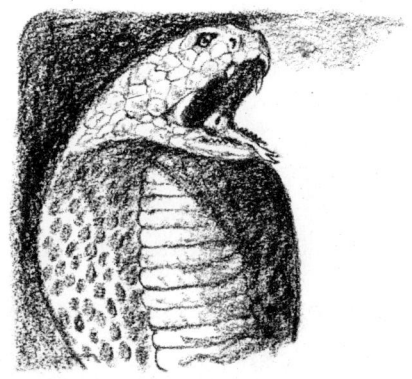

4

The Voice from the Burning Bush

Exodus 3—4

MOSES was leading Jethro's sheep and goats through the wilderness near the great mountain of Sinai. It was such a rocky place that he needed his shepherd's rod to keep the animals from falling.

On the lower side of the mountain he noticed a flame rising from the middle of a bush. The bush was on fire. It was burning bright and red. But it wasn't burning up!

"What a sight!" said Moses to himself. "Why isn't that bush burning up? I'll go take a look."

As he went near, a voice called to him from the middle of the burning bush, "Moses! Moses!"

"Here I am!" he answered.

"Don't come any closer!" warned the voice. "Take off your sandals, for you are standing on holy ground!"

Moses took off his sandals. This was a message from God!

The voice continued, "I am the God of your

ancestors, the God of Abraham, Isaac, and Jacob."

Moses covered his face. He was afraid to look at God.

"I have heard the cries of my people," said the voice from the burning bush. "I have seen their misery. I know how cruelly the Egyptians treat them, and I have come down to save them. I'm going to bring them out of Egypt and take them to the rich and fertile land of Canaan, a land flowing with milk and honey. Come! I will send you to Pharaoh to lead my people out of Egypt!"

"Who, me?" said Moses. "I can't do that!"

"I will be with you," answered God. "After you have led my people out of Egypt, you will worship me on this mountain. That will be the sign that God has sent you."

Moses said, "If I go to the Israelites and tell them that the God of their ancestors has sent me, they'll ask me who you are. What should I say? Tell me your name!"

"I Am who I Am," God answered. "My name, Yahweh, means I Am eternal, I Am with you. Tell the people I Am has sent you." (In Hebrew, God's name is Yahweh. In English we say "the Lord.")

"Tell the Israelites that the Lord, the God of their ancestors, has decided to rescue them from Egypt and take them to the land of Canaan. Don't worry. They'll listen to you. Then go to Pharaoh and tell him that the Lord, the God of the Hebrews, has appeared to you. Ask him to let the people go for a three-day trip into the desert to worship me."

"The people won't believe me," said Moses.

"What's that in your hand?"

"My shepherd's rod."

"Throw it on the ground."

Moses threw his rod down, and it turned into a snake. He was so afraid, he jumped back from it.

"Reach down and pick it up by the tail."

He did as the Lord said, and the snake turned back into a shepherd's rod.

"Now put your hand inside your robe."

Moses obeyed, and when he took his hand out, the skin was covered with snowy white spots. He had a dreadful disease called leprosy.

"Put your hand back inside your robe," the Lord told Moses.

He did, and this time when he took his hand out, it was as healthy as the rest of his body.

"Do these miracles in front of the people as a sign to show them that I've really appeared to you. If they still don't believe you, then show them a third sign. Get some water from the Nile and pour it onto the ground. It will turn into blood."

"Please, Lord!" answered Moses. "Don't send me! I'm a poor speaker! I talk slowly! I stutter!"

"Who gives a person his mouth?" asked the Lord. "Who makes someone deaf or dumb, seeing or blind? It is I, the Lord! I've made you, Moses, and I'll help you speak. Now go! I'll tell you what to say."

"Please, Lord, send anyone else but me!"

"Well, how about your brother Aaron?" asked the Lord, who was angry now. "Aaron speaks well. At this very moment he's on his way to meet you. Tell him what I've said, and he can speak to the people for you. Now take this shepherd's rod and use it to do the miracles which I've shown you."

Moses finally gave in to the Lord. He returned to Midian to say good-bye to Jethro. He took his wife Zipporah and their sons and set out for Egypt, his shepherd's rod in his hand.

Meanwhile, the Lord told Aaron to go into the desert to meet Moses.

So as one brother went west from Midian, the other came east from Egypt, and they met at Sinai. Aaron was so glad to see Moses he kissed him.

Moses reported everything the Lord had said and done, and the two brothers returned to Egypt together.

5

"Let My People Go!"

Exodus 4—7

WHEN they arrived in Egypt, Moses and Aaron went first to Goshen to meet with the leaders of the Israelites. Aaron told them everything the Lord had said, and Moses used the rod to do the miracles God had given him.

The Israelites saw and believed the signs. The Lord knew and cared about their misery. He had shown his power to Moses, and he was going to rescue them from slavery!

They were so happy they bowed down and worshiped the Lord.

Then Moses and Aaron went to the palace and told Pharaoh, "The Lord, the God of Israel, says, 'Let my people go, so they can worship me.'"

"Who's the Lord?" asked Pharaoh. "Why should I obey him? I don't know the Lord, and I won't let the people go!"

"The God of the Hebrews has appeared to us," they explained. "Please let us travel three days into the desert to worship the Lord our God."

"Moses and Aaron!" shouted Pharaoh, "Why

are you taking the people from their work? You Hebrews are increasing in number—that's bad enough—and now you want to take a three-day vacation! Get those slaves back to work!"

After Moses and Aaron left, Pharaoh thought of a plan to keep the Israelites from bothering him again. Their work was making bricks for buildings, he remembered. To do this, they had to chop up straw and mix it with clay. What would happen if they didn't have any straw to hold the bricks together?

The king called in the Egyptian slave drivers and the Hebrew foremen. "Stop giving straw to the slaves," he told them. "From now on, make them go and gather their own straw. But order them to make just as many bricks as before—not one brick less! They don't work hard enough. That's why they keep asking me to let them go! Well, make them work harder! Keep them busy, and they won't have time to listen to Moses and Aaron and their lies!"

The slave drivers and the foremen gave the people the new orders, and the Israelites began looking all over the land for straw.

"What's the matter with you?" the slave drivers asked the Hebrew foremen. "Why aren't you people making as many bricks now as you did before?" Then they whipped the foremen with their lashes.

The foremen went to Pharaoh to complain. "Why do you treat us like this?" they asked. "The slave drivers don't give us any straw, but they order us to make as many bricks as before. It's impossible, and they beat us for not doing it! It's not fair! We haven't done anything wrong!"

"You're lazy, that's what's wrong!" shouted Pharaoh. "You talk about going to worship your God because you don't want to work! Well, now, get back to work!"

Then the Israelite foremen realized that they were in serious trouble.

Just as they were leaving the palace, they met Moses and Aaron, who were waiting for them.

"May the Lord punish you!" cried the foremen. "You've made Pharaoh and the slave drivers hate us! You've given them an excuse to kill us!"

"O Lord," prayed Moses, "why did you let this happen? Oh, why did you ever send me here? Pharaoh is making things worse than ever for your people, and you aren't doing anything to help them!"

"Give the people a message," said the Lord. "Tell the Israelites I'll rescue them from slavery, I'll adopt them as my people, and I'll be their God! When they realize that the Lord is their Savior, I'll take them to the land I promised to Abraham, Isaac, and Jacob and give it to them for their own!"

Moses took the message to the Israelites, but they wouldn't listen to him. They were so crushed by cruel slavery that they couldn't believe the Lord's message.

Then the Lord told Moses and Aaron to go back to Pharaoh.

"The Israelites won't listen to me," said Moses. "Why should Pharaoh listen to me?"

"You'll see," answered the Lord. "First I'll make Pharoah stubborn, and then I'll do miracles in Egypt, I'll strike Pharaoh with my mighty hand, and I'll deliver my people with my outstretched arm! I'll force Pharaoh to let the people go! He'll drive them out! I'm doing this so the Egyptians will realize that I am the Lord!"

So Moses and Aaron went back to the palace, and this time Aaron threw down his rod in front of Pharaoh and all his officials. It turned into a snake.

Pharaoh called for his wise men and magicians, and they threw down their rods, too. Their rods also turned into snakes. But then Aaron's rod swallowed theirs!

Still Pharaoh wouldn't listen. The Lord hardened his heart, and he became too stubborn to let the people go. Then God used his power to strike the Egyptians with ten terrible punishments.

6

God Strikes the Egyptians

Exodus 7—10

THE next day Moses and Aaron went down to the river bank to wait for Pharaoh, who came there every morning. When the king arrived, they warned him that God would strike blows at Egypt if he didn't let the people go.

But Pharaoh refused, so Aaron hit the river with his rod, and instantly all the water in the Nile turned to blood. The fish in the river died, and the water smelled so rotten the Egyptians couldn't drink it.

Then Aaron held his rod over all the other

rivers, canals, ponds, and wells until there was blood everywhere in Egypt, even in the water buckets and jars.

The Egyptian magicians tried to do the same thing with their magic spells, and they were able to turn some water into blood.

The Egyptian people dug holes along the bank of the Nile, searching for clean water to drink. But Pharaoh turned away and went back into his palace, trying to ignore the bloody water all over Egypt.

For seven days the water was blood. Then the Lord sent Moses back to Pharaoh to warn him that if he refused again, God would strike his country with another punishment.

When Pharaoh refused to let the people go, Aaron held his rod over all the waters of Egypt, and frogs came out of the rivers and covered the land.

The Egyptian magicians tried to do the same thing, and they were able to bring up a few frogs.

Pharaoh couldn't ignore what the Lord was doing this time. The Nile was so full of frogs that they jumped out of the water and into his palace and the houses of his people. They even hopped into the ovens and bread pans! Frogs hopped into Pharaoh's bedroom and onto his bed, and they even hopped up on him!

He called for Moses and Aaron. "Pray to the Lord to take these frogs away! Then I'll let the people go!"

"All right," said Moses. "You set the time."

"Tomorrow."

"Just as you say. Tomorrow the frogs will be gone. Then you'll see that there's no god like the Lord our God!"

Moses and Aaron left Pharaoh, and Moses prayed to the Lord to take away the frogs. The Lord answered his prayer, and all the frogs died. The Egyptians piled them up in great heaps until the land was filled with the horrible smell of dead frogs.

But as soon as Pharaoh saw that the frogs were dead, he changed his mind.

Then the Lord sent a third punishment. Aaron struck the ground with his rod, and all over Egypt the dust turned into mosquitoes.

The Egyptian magicians tried to copy this, too, but now their magic failed. The buzzing insects were flying everywhere, biting people and animals.

"This is the finger of God!" the magicians cried out to Pharaoh. But he refused to recognize the power of the Lord.

Early the next morning Moses and Aaron met Pharaoh as he was going to the river. "Let my people go!" they said again.

When Pharaoh refused, the Lord sent thick swarms of flies into his palace and the houses of the Egyptians. Flies covered everything, even the ground they walked on!

But while Pharaoh and his people were

bothered by flies, there were no flies in Goshen, where the people of Israel lived. God spared his people so that Pharaoh would know he was the Lord, even in Egypt. He didn't punish his people as he punished the Egyptians.

Then Pharaoh tried to bargain with Moses and Aaron. "Go, worship your God here in this country," he said.

"No," answered Moses. "The Egyptians would be angry if they saw our worship service. We sacrifice animals to the Lord. If the Egyptians saw us killing rams and goats and bulls, they'd stone us to death for hurting their gods! No, we must travel three days into the desert to worship our God, as he has commanded."

"I'll let you go if you don't go very far," offered Pharaoh. "Just pray for these awful flies to go away!"

"As soon as I leave, I'll pray to the Lord," said Moses. "But don't trick us again!"

The Lord answered Moses' prayer and took the flies away from Pharaoh and the Egyptians, so not a single fly was left. But when Pharaoh saw that they were gone, he refused to let the people go.

The next day the Lord struck the herds of the Egyptians with a terrible disease, so all the horses, donkeys, camels, cattle, and sheep became dreadfully sick, and many died. Pharaoh was amazed to hear that none of the Israelites' animals were sick, but he still wouldn't let the people go.

Then Moses took a few handfuls of ashes from a furnace, stood in front of Pharaoh, and threw the ashes into the air. They spread all over Egypt like dust, and they made big ugly sores called boils break out on the skin of the people and the animals.

This time the Egyptian magicians couldn't even come out to try their spells. They were covered all over with boils, too.

But Pharaoh still refused to let the Hebrew people go.

Then the Lord said to Moses, "Tell Pharaoh that I could wipe him and his people off the face of the earth, but I let them live so they can see my power and tell people everywhere about me."

Early the next morning Moses met Pharaoh and warned him to bring in his animals and everything else which was out in the open fields. Some of Pharaoh's officials were afraid, and they rushed to bring in their servants and animals. Others paid no attention and left everything outdoors.

Then Moses raised his hand toward the sky, and the Lord sent a violent hailstorm, with loud thunder and fiery lightning flashing back and forth. It was the worst storm that anyone could remember. Heavy hail fell on everything that was left out in the open. It beat down on people and animals and killed them. It crushed all the flax and barley plants in the fields and broke down all the trees. There was hail everywhere, except in Goshen.

Finally, Pharaoh sent for Moses and Aaron.

"This time I've sinned," he said. "I'm wrong and the Lord is right. Pray to him. We can't stand any more of his thunder and hail. I'll let you go, I promise. You won't have to stay here one more day."

"As soon as I leave the city," Moses answered, "I'll lift up my hands in prayer to the Lord, and the storm will stop. Then you'll realize that the earth belongs to the Lord!"

Moses left Pharaoh and went out of the city to pray, and the rain and the thunder and the hail stopped, but when Pharaoh saw that the storm was over, he changed his mind again.

Moses and Aaron came back with another warning. "How long will you refuse to humble yourself before the Lord?" they asked.

Pharaoh's officials began to worry. After Moses and Aaron left the palace, they asked the king, "How long is this man Moses going to bring danger to us? Why don't you let just the Israelite men go? Can't you see that Egypt is being ruined?"

Pharaoh agreed to call Moses and Aaron back. "Go, serve the Lord," he said to them, "But tell me, exactly who needs to go?"

"All of us," answered Moses. "Young and old, men and women, sheep and cattle. We need to take all the people and all our animals to worship the Lord."

"Impossible! I'll never let all of you go!" Pharaoh was very angry. "I can see that you're up to something! If you really want to worship, go and take the men with you!"

Then Pharaoh's guards drove Moses and Aaron out of the palace.

The Lord said to Moses, "Raise your hand over the land of Egypt to bring the grasshoppers!"

Moses raised his hand with the rod in it, and

the Lord brought a wind roaring in from the east. It blew on the land all day and all night, and with the wind came hundreds and thousands of grasshoppers. By morning they were swarming all over Egypt.

Nobody had ever seen so many grasshoppers! They filled the houses and covered the land until the ground was black with them. They ate everything—the plants, all the fruit on the trees—every green thing left from the hailstorm was now destroyed by the grasshoppers. Not a single green leaf was left in the whole country.

Pharaoh called for Moses and Aaron to come quickly. "I've sinned against you and against the Lord your God," he admitted. "Now forgive me just this once and pray to your God to take away this deadly punishment!"

The Lord changed the east wind into a strong west wind, which picked up the grasshoppers and blew them into the Red Sea. Not one grasshopper was left in Egypt, but again Pharaoh changed his mind.

Then Moses raised his hand toward the sky, and the Lord sent the ninth punishment. Suddenly, the sun was blotted out by a thick darkness. It was so dark that the Egyptians couldn't see each other, and nobody left home for three days.

In the land of Goshen the sun was shining as usual, and the Israelites came and went as they pleased.

"All right," Pharaoh said when he called Moses. "You may go and serve the Lord. You may even take your women and children. Just leave your animals here."

"Impossible!" answered Moses. "We must take our animals to sacrifice to the Lord. We won't leave a single hoof behind!"

When his last offer was refused, Pharaoh became very angry. "Get out of my sight!" he screamed. "Don't let me ever see your face again! If you show up here, I'll have you killed!"

"Whatever you say," answered Moses. "That's fine with me!"

The Blood of the Lamb

Exodus 11—13

THE Lord had one last message for Pharaoh. "Israel is my firstborn son," he said. "I have told you to let my son go, so he may worship me. You have refused to let him go, so I will kill your firstborn sons."

After Moses announced this last and most terrible punishment, he left the palace and went to Goshen.

He explained God's message to the Israelites. The Lord was going to strike a terrible blow that would make Pharaoh throw them out of Egypt.

He was going to send the Angel of Death through the land at midnight to kill every firstborn son.

But while many Egyptians would die, all the Israelites would be safe. Not even a dog would growl at them, if they followed God's instructions.

First, they must take a perfect young lamb and kill it at sundown without breaking its bones.

"Smear the blood of the lamb over the tops and sides of the door frames of your houses," Moses explained. "When the Angel of Death sees the blood, he'll pass over you and let you live. But remember: no one must go outdoors until morning. Roast the lamb, eat it quickly, then fasten your belts and put on your sandals. You must be ready at a moment's notice to leave for a long, long journey."

The people bowed down and worshiped the Lord, and then they went home and did just as he commanded. They were careful to stay indoors, away from the Angel of Death. They ate the lamb, dressed in their traveling clothes, and sat down to wait.

At midnight they heard loud screams. The Angel of Death was passing through Egypt, killing all the firstborn sons, from Pharaoh's son in the palace to the son of the poorest man in the land. All the firstborn of the animals were killed, too.

But when the angel saw the blood smeared on the door frames of the Israelites' houses, he passed over them and let their sons live. Inside, they waited—listening, trembling.

In the middle of the night Pharaoh got up and found his firstborn son dead. He recognized the power of God, and while it was still dark, he sent for Moses.

"Leave us!" he cried when Moses arrived at the palace. "Get out of here, all of you! Go! Take your children and your animals and go serve your Lord!"

Then, as Moses was leaving, Pharaoh called after him, "Before you go, ask your Lord to bless me, too."

Pharaoh wasn't the only one who wanted the Israelites to leave. The Egyptian people had noticed that while their sons were dying, nothing was hurting the Israelites.

"We'll all be killed!" they said to each other. "Who knows what might happen next? These Israelites mustn't stay here one more day!"

They went to the Israelites during the night to urge them to hurry up and get out. They finally realized that the Lord was watching over his people, and some of them asked the Israelites if they could join them.

The Lord didn't want his people to leave Egypt empty-handed, so he caused some of the Egyptians to give the Israelites fine clothing and gold and silver jewelry.

Early the next morning the nation of Israel marched out of Egypt like a conquering army, carrying great wealth away with them. Thousands of men, women, and children, along with a large number of animals, walked out, right in front of the Egyptians, who were burying their firstborn sons.

They followed Moses out of the city of Rameses and made their way south to Succoth. Since they had left so quickly, they hadn't had time to make bread, so they picked up the bread dough in their baking pans and took it along with them. On the way they stopped to bake. They had left before the yeast was added to the dough, so they baked flat bread instead of the light, fluffy bread they were used to eating.

Every year afterward, when they remembered that day, the Israelites baked their bread without yeast.

"Never forget this day," Moses told them as they walked along. "When you get to the land where the Lord is leading us, celebrate this day. When your children ask what it means, tell them it's the Lord's Passover. Celebrate it to honor him and to remember how he caused the Angel of Death to pass over you in Egypt. He took the blood of the lamb as the price of your freedom. He ransomed you from slavery and brought you out of Egypt with his mighty hand!"

Exactly four hundred and thirty years after Jacob's family had entered Egypt, the Israelites were leaving, carrying Joseph's coffin with them. Just as he had promised, God was rescuing his people.

Crossing the Sea

Exodus 13—15

THE shortest way from Egypt to Canaan was along the main road, by the coast of the Great Western Sea. That would be the fastest way for the Israelites to get to the Promised Land. But the Egyptians had forts on the seacoast, so the Lord didn't lead them that way.

"If the Israelites go the short way," the Lord thought to himself, "they'll have to pass by those forts, and the Egyptian soldiers will attack them. They'll be so scared they'll want to turn around and go back to Egypt."

So he took them around the long way instead, through the desert toward the Red Sea.

They left Succoth and camped at Etham, on the edge of the desert. As they journeyed, they could see the Lord with them, showing them the way to go and giving them light to travel by. During the day the Lord appeared in front of them as a pillar of cloud. At night he appeared as a pillar of fire. When the pillar stopped, it was a sign for them to stop, too, and pitch their tents. When the pillar moved forward, they knew it was time for them to pull down their tents and march on.

At Etham Moses gave the people a message from the Lord: "Turn around and set up camp between the mountains and the Red Sea," he said. "Pharaoh will think you're wandering around lost in the desert, trapped between the mountains and the sea, and he'll try to catch you. I'll defeat him and his army, so the Egyptians will know once and for all that I am the Lord!"

The Israelites turned back and camped by the marshland at the northern end of the Red Sea.

Meanwhile, back at the palace, Pharaoh was changing his mind again. Several days had passed and his officials were complaining.

"What have we done!" they cried. "Why have we let those Hebrew slaves get away?"

Pharaoh ordered six hundred of his best war chariots and horses and drivers to lead the chase after the Israelites to capture them or kill them.

The Egyptian army soon caught up with the

runaway slaves at their camp by the sea. When the Israelites saw the cloud of dust kicked up by the horses, and when they heard the thunder of the chariots, they knew that they were trapped.

They cried out in terror to the Lord, and they complained to Moses, "Weren't there enough tombs in Egypt? Why did you bring us all the way out here to die? We told you this would happen! We told you to leave us alone and let us be slaves. It's better to be a slave in Egypt than to die in this desert!"

"Don't be afraid," said Moses. "Stand still and watch how the Lord will save you today. You're seeing the Egyptians for the last time! The Lord will fight for you! All you have to do is be still."

Then the Lord said to Moses, "Tell the people to stop crying and complaining. Pull up your tent pegs! Get ready to move on!"

The pillar of cloud then moved behind the Israelites, so it was between them and the Egyptians. It brought darkness to the Egyptians, but it gave light to the Israelites, and it kept the two armies separated all night.

Then the Lord told Moses, "Lift up your rod and hold your hand out over the sea."

Moses held his hand out over the sea, and the Lord drove back the water with a strong east wind. The wind blew all night, turning the sea into dry land.

In the morning the sea was divided, and Moses and the Israelites began to move forward on a path of dry land.

When the Egyptians saw the Israelites going right through the middle of the sea, with walls of water on both sides of them, they moved forward, too. Horses, chariots, drivers, and foot soldiers chased after the Israelites right into the sea.

Just before sunrise the fire and cloud came down onto the Egyptian army, throwing them into a panic. The Egyptians tried to turn around, but the Lord clogged their chariot wheels with mud, so they could hardly move.

"The Lord is fighting for the Israelites against us!" they cried in terror. "Let's get out of here!"

Then the Lord told Moses, "Hold your hand out over the sea, and the waters will flow back over the Egyptians."

Moses held out his hand, and just as the sun was rising, the water returned and flowed back, covering Pharaoh's horses, chariots, and drivers. As the Egyptians struggled to escape, the Lord swept them into the sea. Pharaoh's whole army had followed the Israelites, and now they were all drowned. Not one soldier was left alive.

While the Egyptians were drowning, the Israelites were walking through the middle of the sea on dry ground! They passed safely across to the other side. As they looked back, they saw Egyptian soldiers lying dead on the seashore. They realized what the Lord had done for them, and they began to fear him and to trust him and his servant, Moses.

Moses and the Israelites were so full of joy that they celebrated by singing a song of victory. They shouted and sang praises to the Lord for saving his people from the power of the Egyptians. They thanked him for using his great power to rescue them from Pharaoh and from the sea.

> The Lord is our savior!
> He has rescued us from Egypt!
> He is our God!
> We praise him!

The Lord is a warrior!
He has destroyed the enemy!
He guides his people!
The Lord will be king forever and ever!

Then the prophetess Miriam, sister of Moses and Aaron, took her tambourine and led the women in singing the chorus. They followed her, dancing to the sound of tambourines.

Sing to the Lord, for he has won a great victory!
The horse and his rider he has thrown into the sea!

God Makes an Agreement with His People

THE WORLD OF MOSES

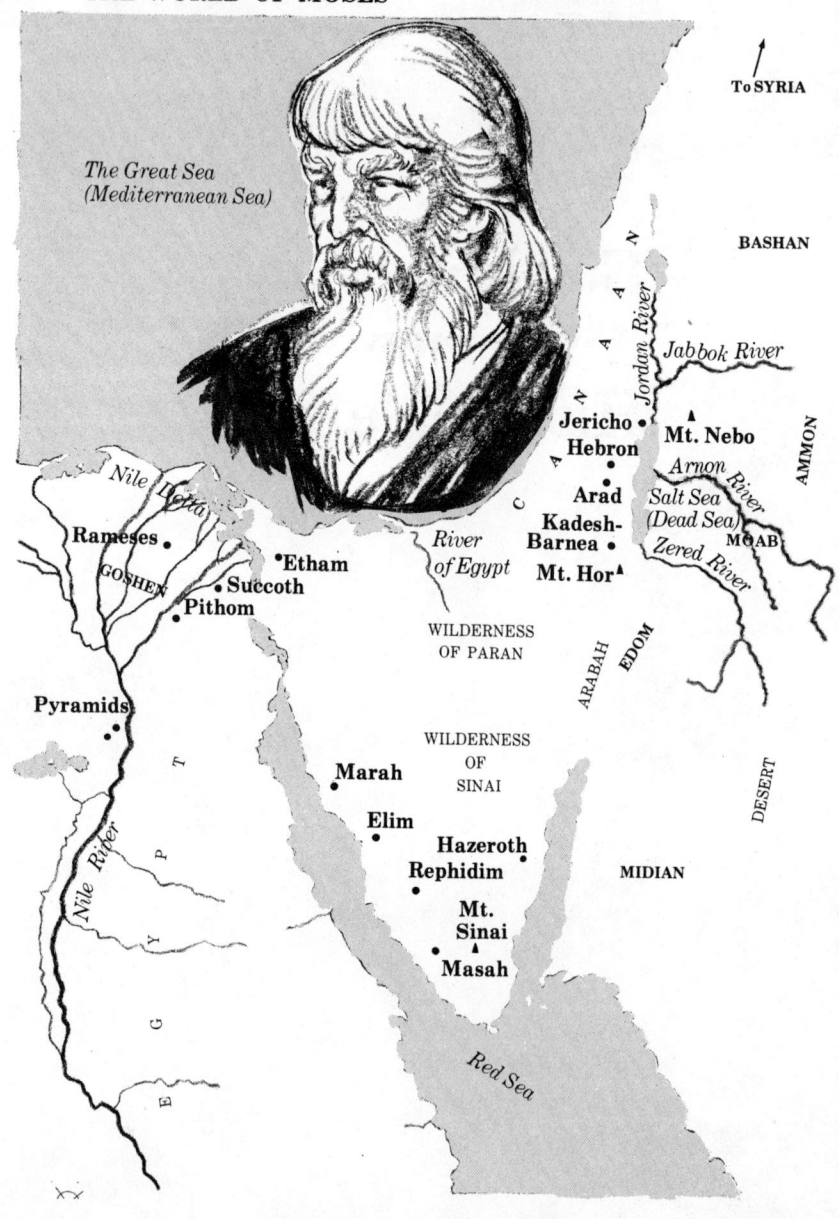

9

Bread from Heaven

Exodus 15—16

AFTER they escaped from Egypt, the people of Israel followed Moses out into the desert on the other side of the sea. Here they found themselves in a rough and rocky wilderness of hills and mountains and bare valleys, quite different from the rich, black earth and flat green fields of Egypt. There were just a few springs of water in this wilderness, and they were scattered many miles apart.

For three days the Israelites walked in the desert without finding anything to drink. They wandered like sheep over the bare rocks, looking for water. Their mouths were dry, the children were crying, and even the animals were thirsty.

Then on the third day they came to an oasis, a pleasant shady place in the desert. They ran forward to drink, but the water was so bitter they spit it out of their mouths. That's why that oasis was called Marah (which means "bitter").

"What are we going to drink?" they asked Moses.

Moses cried to the Lord for help, and the Lord showed him a log and told him to throw it into the bitter water. As soon as he did, the water lost its bad taste and became sweet enough for the people to drink.

While they were camped at Marah, Moses gave the people a warning from the Lord: "Listen to me!" said the Lord. "If you pay attention to my words, if you obey me, I won't punish you as I punished the Egyptians, for I am the Lord, your healer."

Later on the Israelites were sorry that they didn't pay attention to this warning.

They left Marah and walked on until they came to a beautiful oasis named Elim. Here they set up their tents beside twelve springs of sweet water and rested in the shade of seventy palm trees.

From Elim they went on into the desert, a wasteland with no food or water. The Israelites were not used to trusting God, and they began to grumble and complain to each other about Moses and Aaron. They had been away from Egypt for more than a month, and all they had to eat was a little milk and cheese from their sheep and goats.

"The Lord should have killed us in Egypt!" they complained to Moses. "When we were slaves, at least we could sit around our cooking fires and eat as much meat as we wanted! But now you've brought us into this desert, and we're starving!"

What could Moses do?

"I've heard the people's complaints," the Lord told him. "Tell them they'll have all the food they can eat tomorrow morning. I'm going to rain bread down from heaven so they'll know that I am the Lord their God! Tell them to go out every day and gather the food that will come from the sky. I'll give them their daily bread every day for six days. Tell them to gather one day's supply for five days, two day's supply on the sixth day, and nothing on the seventh day. I'm testing them to see whether or not they'll obey me."

Moses and Aaron told the people, "The Lord will give you all the bread you can eat every morning. He has heard your complaints. You're not complaining against us—for who are we?—but against him!"

Suddenly, while Aaron was still speaking, the glory of the Lord appeared out in the desert, looking like a bright light in a cloud!

The next morning when they woke up, the people found a layer of dew all around the camp.

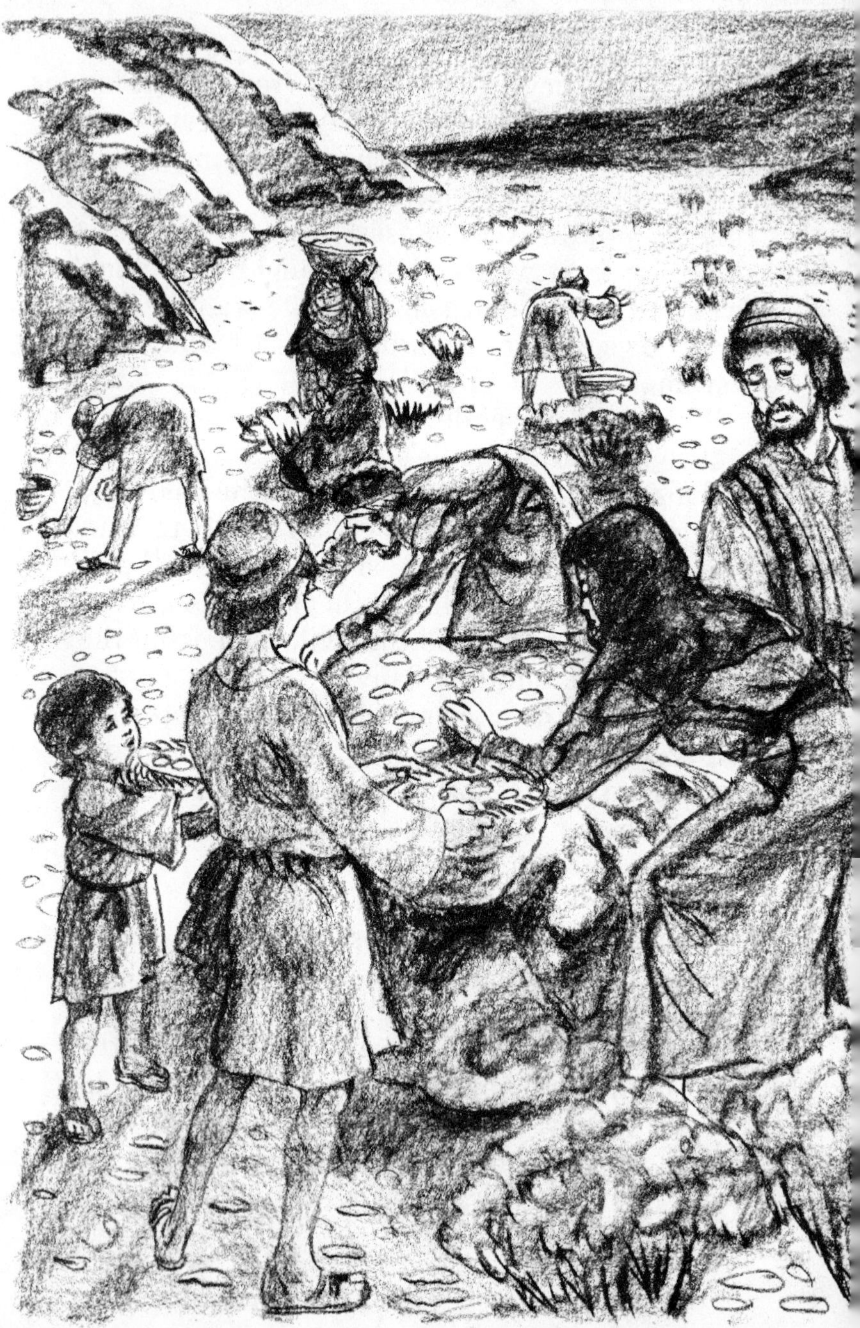

When it dried up, they saw something strange on the ground—something fine and white and powdery, like frost, and round and thin, like a cracker.

"Manna?" they asked, which is Hebrew for "What is it?"

"It's the bread from heaven," answered Moses. "It's the food the Lord is giving you! He says to take as much as you need."

The people gathered the bread from heaven, which they called manna, and filled their baskets with it. Some gathered more, some less, but when they measured it, each one had just as much as he needed!

The manna tasted sweet, like honey bread, and they ground it up and boiled it and made it into cakes and ate it with the milk and cheese.

"Don't keep any for tomorrow," said Moses.

But some of the people didn't pay any attention to him. They saved some of the manna, and the next morning it was full of worms and it smelled rotten. When Moses found out what they had done, he was angry with them.

Each morning after that the manna fell with the dew, and the people gathered only as much as they needed. Later in the day, when the sun got hot, what was left on the ground melted away.

On the sixth day Moses told the people to gather twice as much manna as usual. "The Lord has commanded that tomorrow will be a day of rest," he explained. "It's the sabbath, a day set apart to honor the Lord. Don't do any work tomorrow, but cook and bake enough today to use on the sabbath."

They did what Moses said, and this time the manna they kept overnight didn't spoil or get wormy.

"Rest today," Moses said the next morning, but some of the people still didn't believe him or trust God, and they went out on the sabbath to look for manna.

They didn't find any.

"How long will the Israelites refuse to obey me?" the Lord asked Moses. "Tell them to gather and cook the bread from heaven for six days and to rest on the seventh day, for I have given them the sabbath."

From that time until they entered the Promised Land forty years later, the people of Israel gathered manna according to the Lord's command.

10

Water from a Rock

Exodus 17

THE Israelites came to the oasis of Rephidim, where they set up their tents in the shade. Every morning they found manna on the ground, but no drinking water.

They began to argue with Moses. "Give us water to drink!" they cried.

"Why are you complaining? Why are you testing the Lord?" Moses asked them.

But the people were terribly thirsty and they kept on grumbling. "Why did you bring us out of Egypt? Did you want to let us die of thirst? What about our children and our animals?"

"What should I do with these people?" Moses cried out to the Lord. "They're so angry, they're ready to throw stones at me."

"Take some of the leaders of the Israelites and go on ahead," the Lord answered. "Take your rod with you and go to a large rock I will show you. Strike the rock, and I will make water pour out—enough for all the people and their animals to drink."

Moses did as the Lord said and went on ahead and found the rock and struck it with his rod. Instantly, water gushed from the rock. It poured out over the ground, rushing and bubbling across the dry stones. The leaders called the people to come and drink.

Moses named that place Masah, meaning "test," because the Israelites had tested the Lord by asking whether he was with them.

While they were still camped at Rephidim, a fierce desert tribe from the north, called the Amalekites, sneaked up on them and attacked and killed some of the Israelites.

Moses called Joshua, a young man who was his helper. "Pick out some men to go fight the Amalekites," he said.

Joshua chose some men, and the next day they marched out to fight the Amalekites.

Moses and his brother Aaron and another leader named Hur went to the top of a nearby hill to watch the battle. Moses stood with his arms stretched out, his rod in one hand. As long as he held up his arms as in prayer, the Israelites beat the Amalekites, but as soon as he let his arms down, the Amalekites began to win. When his arms began to ache and feel heavy, Aaron and Hur found a large stone for Moses to sit on, and they stood on either side of him and held up his arms.

The three men stayed on top of the hill until evening. Aaron and Hur held Moses' arms steady while Joshua completely defeated the Amalekites.

Then the Lord said to Moses, "Write down what happened so the people will remember," and Moses wrote down the story of the battle. Then he built an altar and offered thanksgiving to the Lord for the victory over the Amalekites.

11

The Ten Commandments

Exodus 19—20

THREE months after they left Egypt, the Israelites set up camp in the wilderness near Mount Sinai, the great rocky mountain where Moses had heard the voice from the burning bush. Here the Israelites met the Lord.

Moses left the people in the camp and climbed up the great mountain that rose from the bare, flat wilderness. The Lord gave him a message to bring back to the people.

"You saw what I did to the Egyptians," said the Lord. "You saw how I carried you as a mother eagle carries her children on her wings, and how I brought you to this place. If you obey me now, I'll take you for my people. Everything on earth is mine, but you'll belong to me in a special way. You'll be my chosen people, a kingdom of priests, a holy nation, set apart from other nations to serve me."

When the people heard the message, they said, "We'll do whatever the Lord tells us to do."

Moses returned to the mountain and reported to the Lord that the Israelites wanted to obey him and be his people.

"Listen!" said the Lord, "In three days I am coming down on to the top of Mount Sinai, in a thick dark cloud. The people will see the cloud and hear me talking to you, and they'll trust you. But first they must get ready. Tell them to clean themselves and wash their clothes. They must stay away from the mountain until they hear a long blast on a trumpet. Then they must come near the mountain, but warn them not to touch it. It is forbidden, holy ground."

Moses returned to the people and told them to get ready to meet the Lord. They washed themselves and their clothes, and on the morning of the third day they heard loud thunder rolling and crashing on the mountain. They looked up and saw flashes of lightning, and then a huge, dark cloud came down and covered the mountaintop.

Suddenly they heard a long, loud blast, the

sound of a trumpet made from a ram's horn. All the people in the camp trembled with fear, and they left their tents and followed Moses until they stood at the foot of Mount Sinai.

By now the entire mountain was completely covered with smoke. The glory of the Lord was coming down on top of it in the form of fire, and smoke was rising up, so Mount Sinai looked like a giant furnace. The whole mountain shook and trembled like a volcano about to erupt.

The sound of the trumpet grew louder and louder. Moses spoke, and God answered him in a voice like thunder, warning the people not to come up the mountain.

Then Moses stood down below with the people and listened while God spoke the words of the Ten Commandments:

"I am the Lord your God who brought you out of Egypt, the land of slavery.

"You must not make idols or worship other gods.

"You must not use my name carelessly.

"Remember to keep the sabbath day separate from other days. Work for six days and rest on the seventh day, for in six days I created heaven and earth, and on the seventh day I rested.

"Honor your father and mother, and you will live a long time in the land which I will give to you.

"You must not kill.

"You must not be unfaithful to your husband or wife.

"You must not steal.

"You must not tell a lie about anyone.

"You must not wish you had things that belong to other people."

As God spoke, the people heard the thunder and the loud trumpet blasts, and they saw the fiery lightning and the smoke coming from the top of the mountain. Trembling with fear, they backed away and stood at a distance.

"Tell us what God says, and we'll listen," they told Moses, "but don't let God speak to us like this, or we'll die!"

"Don't be afraid," answered Moses. "God is showing his great and terrible power so you'll obey him."

But the people were afraid to come near the mountain, and they kept their distance.

12

An Agreement Signed in Blood

Exodus 20—24

MOSES left the people and went up alone into the thick dark cloud where God was. The Lord told him to say to the people: "You've heard me speaking to you from heaven. Now do as I say. Worship me, and I will be with you, and I will bless you."

Then he gave Moses instructions about treating people fairly, about being kind to foreigners, and about helping enemies and poor people.

"Pay attention to everything I have told you," said the Lord. "Obey me, and I will drive away all your enemies. Don't worship idols, and I will bless you. Serve me, and I will give you everything you need."

Moses wrote down all the words of the Lord, and early the next morning he got up and built an altar at the foot of the mountain and offered some bulls as sacrifices. He took the blood of the animals and put half of it into bowls and threw the other half against the altar. Then he read aloud to the people what the Lord had said.

The people answered, "We'll obey the Lord and do everything he commands."

Then Moses took the bowls and splashed the rest of the blood at the people, saying, "This is the blood of the covenant which the Lord has made with you."

A covenant is a kind of agreement between people or nations. This covenant was an agreement between God and the Israelites. Spilling blood was a way of signing the covenant, of promising to keep it. The Lord was promising to be their God, and they were promising to obey him.

After the covenant-making, Moses went back up the mountain. This time he took along Aaron and his two oldest sons and seventy of the leaders of the people. On their way up, they had a vision of the God of Israel. They saw something that looked like a smooth floor of blue jewels under God's feet, and it was as bright and clear as heaven itself!

They bowed down and worshiped, and then they ate and drank together on the mountainside.

"Wait here," Moses told the others. "I'm going further up the mountain. Let Aaron and Hur be in charge while I'm gone."

Then he climbed up to the top of Mount Sinai. As the others watched, Moses disappeared into the thick cloud that covered the mountain top.

Moses' helper, Joshua, stayed on the mountainside, and the other leaders went back to the camp.

Then the glory of the Lord came down and

rested on the mountain. To the people at the bottom, it looked as though a fire was burning on the top of Mount Sinai.

For six days the cloud covered the mountain, and on the seventh day the Lord called to Moses from the middle of the cloud. Moses went into the cloud and stayed there for forty days and forty nights.

The Story of the Golden Calf

Exodus 32

WHERE was Moses?

The Israelites didn't know. Forty days had passed, and still their leader had not returned. Was he lost in the thick dark cloud on the top of Mount Sinai? Was he dead? They didn't know, and they were tired of waiting.

The people gathered around Moses' brother, Aaron. "Come on!" they shouted. "Make a god to lead us! That man Moses who led us out of Egypt—who knows what has happened to him? He has disappeared!"

"All right," answered Aaron. "If you need an image of God, then take off your golden earrings and bring them to me."

The people took off the golden earrings they had been wearing since they left Egypt and brought them to Aaron.

He took the earrings and melted them down in the campfire. Then he formed the lump of gold into the shape of a young bull. The golden calf he made looked a lot like the idols which the Egyptians worshiped.

"Here's our god, O Israel!" shouted the people. "Here's the god who led us out of Egypt!"

When Aaron heard the shouts, he built an altar in front of the golden calf.

"Tomorrow we'll have a feast to honor the Lord," he said, thinking that the people just wanted an image they could see in order to worship the Lord. He was wrong.

Early the next morning the people brought animals to offer as sacrifices to the golden calf. They sat down to eat and drink, and the feast soon turned into a wild party, with the people behaving like the idol worshipers of Egypt.

All this time, the mountain was smoking and thundering above them.

Up on the mountaintop, the Lord was speaking to Moses. "Hurry on down, for your people are sinning!"

Moses hurried down the mountainside, carrying two large stone tablets with God's laws written on both sides. God himself had made them and he had written on them with his finger.

Part way down the mountain Moses met Joshua.

"Listen! I hear the sound of battle in the camp!" cried Joshua.

"No," answered Moses when he heard the people shouting below. "That's not the sound of victory that I hear, nor the sound of defeat. That's the sound of singing that I hear!"

As he came further down the mountainside, Moses saw the Israelite camp and the golden calf with the people dancing and singing around it.

He was so furious he threw the stone tablets of the Law down at the foot of the mountain, and they shattered to pieces on the rocks.

As he stormed into the camp, the singing and dancing stopped. In the silence, Moses seized the golden calf and threw it into the fire. It melted back into a lump of gold. Then he ground the gold into a fine powder, mixed it with water, and forced the people to drink it, as punishment. The ones who had worshiped the idol were made sick and died.

Next he turned to Aaron.

"What have these people done to you, that you've made them commit such a terrible sin?" he demanded.

"Don't be angry with me, Moses! You know how wicked these people are! They got tired of waiting for you to return. They asked me to make them a god to lead them, so I took their gold jewelry and threw it into the melting pot on the fire, and, well—out came this calf!"

Moses went to the gate of the camp and shouted, "Everyone who's on the Lord's side, come over here and stand by me!"

His own tribe, the Levites, came and stood by him. "Punish the idol worshipers!" Moses told them. "Take your swords and go through the camp and kill them all!"

The Levites obeyed Moses and went through the camp with their swords, and they killed about three thousand people.

"You Levites have been loyal to the Lord," Moses told them. "He'll reward you for this!"

14

God Gives the People Another Chance

Exodus 32—34

THE next day Moses told the people, "You've committed a great sin, but I'll go back to the Lord and ask him to forgive you."

As he climbed back up the mountain, his heart was full of grief and sadness. "O Lord," he moaned when he reached the top, "Please listen to me! Your people have done a terrible thing, but please forgive them!"

"They've disobeyed me!" said the Lord. "They've broken my laws! I'm so angry, I'm ready to destroy all of them!"

"O Lord, please don't be angry with your people! Don't destroy them! Remember your promises!"

"They're not my people anymore," said the Lord. "I'll make you and your descendants my people instead!"

"If you won't forgive your people, Lord, then erase my name from the book where you've written down the names of your people."

"If I erase any names," answered the Lord, "they'll be the names of those who have disobeyed me! I'm not going to be with them any more! Go back and lead your people to Canaan without me!"

Moses returned to the people with the bad news. When they heard that the Lord wasn't going to be with them anymore, they began to weep, and they took off their jewelry as a sign of their sorrow.

Moses went back to the Lord. "You told me to lead the people," he said, "but I don't know how. Teach me your ways."

"Don't worry. I'm sending an angel to guide you and protect you and lead you safely to the land I have prepared for you. Because you're my friend, Moses, and I'm pleased with you, I'll do as you ask."

Moses prayed, "Show me your glory."

Then the Lord came down in the form of a cloud and stood there with Moses. He put Moses in a crack in a large rock and covered him with

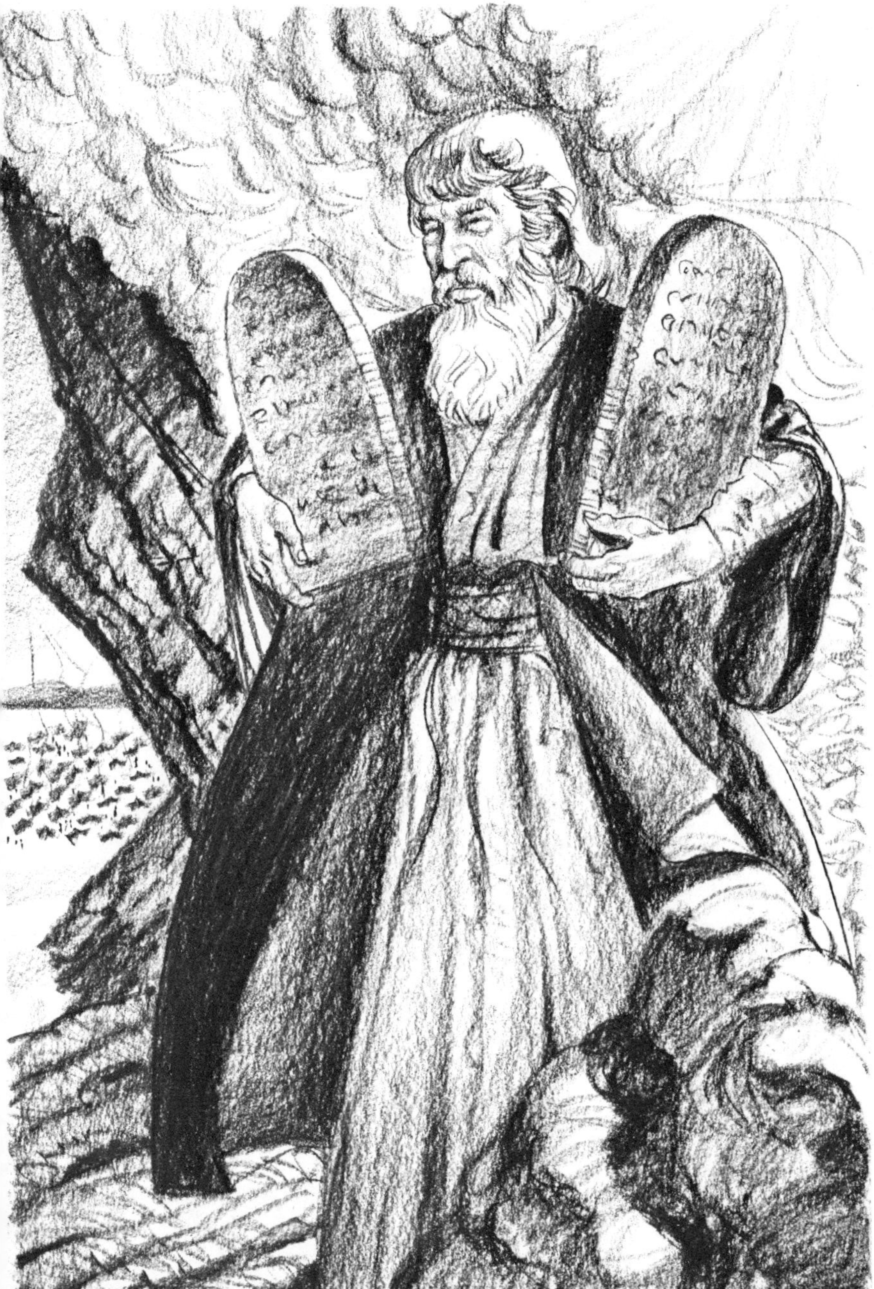

his hand. He called out his name, Yahweh, meaning "I am with you."

Then he passed in front of Moses, saying, "I am the Lord God, full of goodness and mercy, slow to anger, faithful and loving, forgiving and merciful, but I do not let evil go unpunished."

Moses bowed down to the ground and worshiped the Lord. He prayed, "O Lord, if you're really pleased with me, go with us! Don't make us go without you! How will anyone know we're your people unless you're with us? If you're not with us, then we're just like all the other nations in the world. Please forgive our sins! Please let us be your own special people again!"

"All right," answered the Lord. "I will forgive the people and give them my laws again, the laws that they broke by worshiping an idol. If they obey me, I'll do great things for them, things that have never been seen in this world! All other nations will see what I do for my people! I'll drive out their enemis and give them the land. But beware of idols! Watch out for their clever traps! I am jealous, and I will not allow my people to worship other gods!"

Then Moses cut two stone tablets like the first ones, and the Lord wrote the same Ten Commandments on them.

Moses spent another forty days and nights up on the mountaintop with the Lord, neither eating nor drinking, and this time the people waited patiently for him.

Finally, he came down the mountain. Aaron and the others saw him coming with the new set of stone tablets in his hands, but when they looked at his face, they were afraid to go near him.

Moses didn't realize it, but his face was shining because he had seen the glory of the Lord in a way that no other human being ever had before.

Moses called out to them, and Aaron and the leaders of the people went to him, and they talked together. Then the rest of the people came up and gathered around him, and Moses gave them God's laws and told them what God had said to him.

When he finished speaking to the people, Moses put a veil over his face. After that, whenever he talked to the Lord, Moses took off the veil, and his face began to shine. When he returned to the people, he told them what the Lord had said. Then he put the veil back over his face, until it was time to talk to the Lord again.

15

God's Tabernacle in the Wilderness

Exodus 25—27; 30—31; 35—40; Leviticus 24

THE Lord wouldn't let his people make idols, but he understood that they needed something to remind them of him. So he gave Moses a plan for a special tent, a place set apart for worship, a house for God among his people.

Since God is spirit, nobody can see him, and he is everywhere at the same time. But the tent helped the Israelites remember that God was with them in a special way.

The people moved God's tent along with the other tents whenever they changed camp.

Everything in it could be taken apart, packed up, and carried.

This tent of God was called the tabernacle.

Moses took up an offering from the people to build the tabernacle.

"Everyone who is willing, give what you can to the Lord," he said. "Bring gold, silver, and copper; colored yarn and cloth; goat's hair and skins; wood and leather; oil, spices, perfume, and jewels. If you're a skilled craftsman, come, help make the tabernacle! We need a tent and furniture, an altar, and special clothing for the priests."

The people searched their tents until they found the cloth and jewelry that the Egyptians had given them on the night of the Passover. They brought everything to Moses: gold pins and rings and necklaces, fine cloth, leather, silver, copper, wood, precious gems, and expensive spices and oils.

They all gave their most valuable possessions for God's tabernacle.

"Look," said Moses. "The Lord has picked Bezalel and Oholiab to make the tabernacle and everything in it. God has given me his plan, with the exact measurements for his tent, and he has given these two men skill in designing, gem cutting, woodcarving, weaving, and embroidering. He has given them the ability to teach others these things, and he has filled them with his spirit."

Bezalel and Oholiab and the other engravers, seamstresses, embroiderers, and weavers came forward and offered their skills for the Lord's work. Moses gave them the things the people had brought, and they got to work, following God's plan.

Every morning the craftsmen were interrupted by people bringing more offerings. Finally, the craftsmen told Moses, "The people are bringing more than we need!"

Moses told the people not to bring anything else. They had already given more than enough to complete the job.

With Bezalel in charge, the craftsmen worked day after day, week after week, month after month—designing and carving, weaving and embroidering, making the tent and its furniture, the courtyard, the altar, and the priests' clothing.

Finally they were finished, and they brought their work to Moses. He inspected everything carefully. It was all made exactly as the Lord had commanded!

Moses was so pleased and happy that he blessed the people.

Then it was time to set up God's tent.

When it was finished, the tabernacle stood in the middle of the camp, with a large open space, called the courtyard, around it.

An enormous linen curtain hung around the outside of the courtyard. The curtain was seven feet high, too high for even the tallest person to look over. It was made of bright blue, purple, and red cloth, beautifully designed and embroidered.

Inside the courtyard stood a copper basin and a wooden altar.

The basin was made from mirrors given by the women. It was to be used for washing by the people who sacrificed at the altar.

The altar was a square box without a top or bottom, a place for burning the offerings which the people brought to the Lord. It was made of wood so it could be carried from place to place, and it was plated with copper to make it fireproof. It had copper rings on the sides and copper-covered wooden poles to go through the rings, for carrying. A copper grating fit on the top, to hold the fire and the offerings, so the ashes could fall through to the ground below.

Along with the altar the craftsmen made pots to carry away the ashes, and shovels, bowls, forks, and fire pans of copper.

The tabernacle was larger than the other tents in the camp, and much more beautiful. It stood at the far end of the courtyard, forty-five feet long, fifteen feet wide, and fifteen feet high, about the size of a large house.

The walls of the tabernacle were made of wooden boards, fastened with hooks so they could be taken down like the people's goathair tents.

Outside, the walls were covered with beautiful hangings of finely woven linen embroidered in bright thread with pictures of cherubs. Inside, the walls were covered with gold.

The front of the tabernacle was open, with a brightly colored cloth curtain for a wall.

The roof of the tabernacle was made of layers of cloth and leather. The floor was bare ground, like the other tents.

The space inside the tabernacle was divided into two rooms by a thick linen curtain called the veil. The veil was embroidered with colorful designs of cherubs. It was fastened to the roof with golden hooks.

The larger, outer room was called the holy place, and the smaller, inner room was called the holy of holies, meaning the most holy place.

Three pieces of furniture inside the holy place were each covered with gold. The golden table held golden dishes and saucers, pitchers and cups, for offerings of bread and wine.

The second piece of furniture in the holy place was a lampstand made of solid gold. It looked like an enormous candlestick, with oil lamps instead of candles on each of its seven branches. Pure olive oil burned in the lamps, so that the golden room was always aglow with the flickering light of the lamps. This light was never allowed to go out.

A sweet-smelling perfume called incense was given off by burning spices and gums on the small gold-covered altar of incense, the third piece of furniture in the Holy Place. The incense filled the golden room with clouds of heavy, perfumed smoke.

Of course God didn't need bread to eat, light to see, or perfume to smell, but these things in the holy place were signs to the Israelites that the Lord their God lived among them.

On the far side of the veil was the dark, mysterious holy of holies, a room fifteen feet square. The holy of holies had only one piece of furniture—a large wooden box covered with gold inside and out. This was the most important object in the tabernacle, the ark of the covenant.

The ark was a chest two feet wide, four feet long, and two feet high. It stood in the middle of the golden room. It had golden rings and gold-plated poles for carrying.

The lid of the ark was made of solid gold, and it was decorated with two golden figures of cherubs. These winged creatures with animal bodies and human heads faced each other, and their outspread wings formed the mercy seat, which was the throne for the invisible King whose house was the tabernacle.

When everything else was set in place, Moses took the two stone tablets of the law, Aaron's rod, and a jar of manna and placed them inside the ark of the covenant. These were Israel's most precious possessions.

It was exactly one year since the day they had left Egypt.

16

Worshiping the Lord

Exodus 28—29; 39; Leviticus 1—9; Numbers 5—8; 18—19; 28—30

BECAUSE God is holy, the Israelites couldn't be his people unless they were holy, too. They needed some way to make things right when they broke God's laws, some way to have their sins forgiven. So after the tabernacle was set up, the Lord gave Moses a plan to help make things right between him and his people.

According to God's plan, priests offered sacrifices and prayers every day at the great altar in the courtyard and at the golden altar of incense in the tabernacle. They brought twelve fresh loaves of bread into the holy place each week, and they kept the oil lamps on the golden lampstands burning.

God chose Aaron and his sons to be the first priests, and for hundreds of years afterward, the grandsons and great-grandsons of Aaron's family served as priests for Israel.

Aaron was the first high priest, in charge of all the other priests. Only the priests were allowed inside the tabernacle, and only the high priest was allowed inside the holy of holies. And he was allowed in that special room only one day a year.

After the tabernacle was set up, Moses called the people together for a special seven-day service to ordain Aaron and his sons as priests.

He poured oil on the priests' heads as a sign that God's spirit was in them. Then he gave them the special robes made by the craftsmen.

Each priest put on a tunic, a sash, and a turban.

The tunic was made of beautiful purple cloth, embroidered with gold and decorated with golden bells sewn into the hem. When the priests went in and out of the tabernacle, the people heard the tinkling of the little golden bells.

On each man's head Moses placed a linen turban with a golden ornament in front engraved with the words, "Holy to the Lord." This reminded everyone that the priests were set apart especially for the Lord's service.

In addition to these priestly clothes, the high

priest wore a breastpiece covered with twelve brightly colored jewels arranged in four rows, with three jewels in each row. He also wore a golden vest with two precious jewels on the shoulders.

The priests wore nothing on their feet, for it was the custom to go barefoot in a holy place.

They wore their splendid robes whenever they served in the tabernacle. At other times they wore regular clothes.

After Aaron and his sons put on their priestly clothes, Moses took special perfumed anointing oil and poured it on the tabernacle and on everything in it—the table, the lampstand, the altar of incense, and the ark of the covenant. Then he anointed the great altar and the basin in the courtyard. This meant that everything was dedicated to the Lord.

Aaron offered sacrifices on the altar, and then he raised his hands and blessed the people, saying, "May the Lord bless you and keep you. May the Lord make his face shine upon you and be gracious to you. May the Lord look kindly upon you and give you peace."

Then the people shared a meal and celebrated.

Moses took Aaron into the tabernacle and they prayed together. Then they came out and blessed the people again.

While they were standing there, the Lord appeared as a pillar of cloud, covering the tabernacle. The glory of the Lord filled the tent, and all the people saw him as a bright and shiny, unearthly light.

As they were staring at the light of God's presence, the Lord sent a fire to the great altar to burn up what was left of Aaron's offering. When the people saw this, they shouted and fell down in joy. The sacrifice was their gift to God, and when God accepted it, they knew he was accepting them, too.

This holy fire from God was never allowed to

go out. Even when they moved camp, the priests were careful not to let God's fire die out. They carried the smoldering embers of the fire in a special fire pan and used these embers to start a new fire at the next camping place. The fire, always burning, was a sign that God's people never stopped worshiping him, but were always offering him prayer and praise.

The fire on the altar was also used to burn the incense on the small golden altar in the tabernacle. The priests carried live coals in a fire pan, being careful to use only the fire lit by the Lord. The burning incense gave off a sweet smell and sent bright blue smoke up to heaven along with the people's prayers.

The priests led worship services twice a day, in the morning and in the evening. They also made special sacrifices on the sabbath and on holidays and when people brought offerings to give thanks or to ask forgiveness.

People brought birds or grain or animals as an offering. They always brought the best they had, a sign that they were giving themselves to the Lord.

Some offerings were eaten, and others were burned up. An animal offered for sin was always killed outside camp.

During the daily services, the priests killed an ox or a lamb, put its blood into a basin, poured the blood over the animal, and burned it on top of the wood on the great altar.

The blood of animals was a powerful offering to take away sin. The people knew that God would accept the blood instead of themselves. Since the life of all living creatures is in the blood, and since God creates life, all life and all blood belong to him. Only a sacrifice of living blood could be offered for sin, to bring God and his people back together as friends.

The Levites helped the priests in the tabernacle and carried the furniture and the tabernacle when they moved camp.

17

Unholy Fire!

Leviticus 10—15

THE Israelites were glad that the Lord had decided to be their God and to live among them. Every morning and every evening Aaron and his sons offered sacrifices at the great altar in the courtyard and burned incense on the golden altar in the tabernacle. The people prayed and sang songs of praise to the Lord.

Since God's people and God's tabernacle were holy, the work of the priests also included keeping everything clean according to special rules. Persons sick with leprosy or sores and those who had touched a dead body had to leave the camp until the priests checked them. The priests offered sacrifices to take away the guilt of this kind of uncleanness. They couldn't make the people pure, or cure disease, or forgive sins, but with the rules of sacrifice they could take away the guilt. Only the Lord himself could forgive sins.

God told his people how to worship him and he gave them rules about health and cleanness so they could be his holy people.

Then one day something terrible happened.

Aaron's two older sons, Nadab and Abihu, came into the holy place to start the fire on the golden altar of incense. They knew God's rule: the fire must come only from the great altar, where God had lit his holy fire. But today for some reason Nadab and Abihu didn't bother to follow the rule. They were probably drunk.

Instead, they took some common, unholy fire, put it in the fire pans, and took it into the holy place.

God was angry at them for disobeying his rule, and for treating the offering of incense without respect. So, while the two young men were still standing by the golden altar in their priestly clothes, the Lord suddenly sent fire out of the altar, and it burned them to death, right there in the holy place.

The people were shocked. What did this terrible thing mean?

Moses explained to Aaron, "The Lord meant what he said. Everyone who serves him must treat him with respect, for he is holy. We must give him honor, or he won't show his glory among his people."

But Aaron could say nothing.

Then Moses sent for their cousins, Mishael and Elzaphan. "Come here and carry your cousins' bodies away from the tabernacle and put them outside the camp."

They came and carried the bodies away.

"Don't mourn for Nadab and Abihu," Moses told Aaron and his two younger sons, Eleazar and Ithamar. "You must stay in the tabernacle and keep on serving the Lord. Let the rest of us cry and mourn for them."

They did as Moses said.

Then the Lord told Aaron, "From now on, you and your sons must not drink wine when you're serving here. All priests must keep this law, so you can tell the difference between holy and unholy things, and so you can teach my ways to the people."

Then Moses told them to offer a sacrifice and eat part of it. Later he came back and discovered that they hadn't done as he had told them, and he was angry.

"Why didn't you do what you should?" he asked them.

"I didn't think it would make any difference," answered Aaron sadly. "We offered sacrifices properly this morning, and look what happened!"

Moses realized how his brother felt, and he left him alone.

18

The Goat That Was Sent Away

Leviticus 16—22

THE daily worship services and sacrifices at the tabernacle were part of God's plan for his people. He also gave them instructions for cleansing themselves of sin in another way. At a special service on the Day of Atonement the high priest entered the holy of holies, offered blood, and received God's forgiveness for the people.

On this special day of the year the high priest dressed in special robes, and the people ate no food and did no work. They brought two goats to the high priest, and he took the animals to the entrance of the tabernacle. One goat was marked "for the Lord," and it was sacrificed on the altar. The other goat was marked "the scapegoat," and it was sent away.

What wonderful relief the Israelites felt when God forgave them and freed them from sin! They watched the high priest go in and out of the tabernacle with great joy and excitement. Something wonderful and mysterious was happening, something that God was doing especially for them. It was atonement, which means wiping away sins.

The high priest took the blood of the goat which was being sacrificed, covered it with incense, and took it into the tabernacle. He walked through the golden holy place, lifted the veil, and stepped into the dark and mysterious holy of holies. There he burned the incense and sprinkled the blood. The blue smoke of the burning incense formed a cloud which covered the mercy seat. Then he sprinkled the mercy seat with blood. The mercy seat over the ark of the covenant was the place of forgiveness, of God's mercy toward his people.

Next the high priest took the scapegoat and put both of his hands on its head and confessed the sins of the people. The sins of the people passed into the scapegoat.

Then the people drove the scapegoat away into the wilderness, carrying all their sins with it. The goat wandered in the desert, never finding its way back to the camp, and the people's sins were gone forever.

This showed the Israelites that God forgave and forgot their sins. In God's mercy, everything that was confessed was sent away and gone forever.

Each year the Israelites repeated this service on the Day of Atonement. The sins of the whole year were taken away by blood and driven into the wilderness, forgiven and forgotten.

The Lord wanted his people to be without sin so they could follow his ways and obey his laws. He wanted them to be holy, set apart from other nations.

"Don't act like other nations," he told them.

"Don't copy the bad behavior of the Egyptians or the Canaanites. I'm disgusted by their evil customs."

He told the people not to lie, cheat, or steal. He wanted them to be fair and to live at peace with everyone.

"Don't stay angry with anyone," he said. "Don't pay anyone back when you're hurt, and don't go on hating. Be kind to foreigners. Remember, you were foreigners in Egypt. Love foreigners as you love your own people, and love your neighbor as you love yourself."

19

A Calendar for God's People

Exodus 23; Leviticus 23—27; Numbers 28—29

GOD told his people to set aside certain days for rest, other days for special worship services, and still other days for celebrations. The Israelites followed this calendar every year.

The seventh day of each week was the sabbath day, a day of rest for the people, to remind them that the earth is the Lord's and that everything he created is complete and good.

Every seventh year was a sabbath year, a year of rest for the land. The people were not to plant or harvest during the sabbath year, but they could eat what the Lord gave them the other six years.

Every fiftieth year was the year of jubilee, when all things were given back to their original owners. This included land, money, and slaves. The nearest relative of a slave was called the redeemer, and he bought back the slave and set him free. Jubilee reminded the people that the land belongs to the Lord, not to them. God allowed them to use the land and to take care of it for him, but they didn't really own it.

Each year the people celebrated five important holidays. In early spring, Passover reminded them of their escape from Egypt. On Passover they ate lamb and flat bread and told the story of how God brought them out of slavery.

Pentecost was seven weeks after Passover. This was the celebration of the gathering of the firstfruits of the spring harvest. The Israelites kept Pentecost after they got to Canaan and planted wheat.

In the fall they celebrated the New Moon, the New Year, and the Day of Atonement.

Another holiday in Canaan was the Feast of Tabernacles, to celebrate the fall harvest of grapes and olives. During the Feast of Tabernacles, the Israelites lived in simple huts made of branches. This reminded them and their children of the time they spent living in tents in the wilderness. This holiday came right after the Day of Atonement.

On these holidays the priests offered extra sacrifices and led special worship services. The people sang and prayed and remembered the many things which the Lord had done for them.

After he explained about the special days, the Lord told Moses what would happen to the people if they obeyed him, and what would happen if they disobeyed.

If they obeyed, the Lord would bless them and give them more than they needed. If they stayed away from idols, they would live peacefully in the Promised Land, and the Lord would live among them and be their God.

If they disobeyed, he would punish them. If they worshiped idols, he would take them away from the land to a foreign country. But even then he would forgive those who were truly sorry and bring them back to the land.

God had rescued the Israelites from Egypt and he had made a covenant with them so they could be his special people. Because he loved them, he wanted his people to follow his teaching and obey his laws. This was the best way for God's people to live.

God Teaches
His People

20

Marching Orders

Exodus 18; Numbers 1—4, 9—10

THE Israelites had camped at Mount Sinai for almost a year, building the tabernacle and learning God's teachings. Now it was time to leave. But before they folded up their tents, the Lord told Moses to count the people.

"Count the Israelites by tribes," he said. "Take a census and find out how many men there are who can go to war. I'll pick a leader from each tribe to help you."

So Moses and Aaron and the leaders of the tribes counted all the men twenty years old and older who could go to war. They counted them by families and tribes, from the twelve tribes of Reuben, Simeon, Judah, Issachar, Zebulun, Benjamin, Dan, Asher, Gad, Naphtali, Manasseh, and Ephraim.

The Lord set apart the tribe of Levi to work in the tabernacle, and since he didn't want them to go to war, they were counted separately. Not including the Levites, there were more than six hundred units of military men in Israel.

Moses' father-in-law, Jethro, heard how God was helping the Israelites, and he came out to visit them. After they greeted each other, they went into Moses' tent and Moses told Jethro how God had brought them out of Egypt, and how he had punished the Egyptians. He told Jethro how the Lord gave them food from heaven, water from a rock, and victory over the Amalekites.

"Blessed be the Lord!" said Jethro. "He has saved you from the power of Pharaoh! He has rescued his people from the Egyptians, who were so mean to them! Now I know that the Lord is greater than all other gods!"

Jethro brought an offering to the Lord, and Aaron and all the leaders of the Israelites joined Jethro and Moses in a meal of thanksgiving to God.

The next day Jethro gave Moses some good advice about sharing more of his work with the other leaders. Moses was weary of settling arguments day after day and teaching the people

God's ways. So he followed Jethro's advice and asked some other leaders to share the work.

One morning the Israelites woke up to discover that the cloud over the tabernacle had lifted. The Lord was telling them that it was time to move on again.

"You've been here at Sinai long enough," he said. "Now go, break camp, and move on toward the land of Canaan. I am giving it to you, as I promised Abraham, Isaac, and Jacob. Now go in and occupy it!"

Then Moses said to Jethro, "The Lord wants us to leave for Canaan. He says he'll give us the land, so come along with us and we'll look after you!"

"No," answered Jethro, "I must go back to my own country."

"Please don't leave us now," said Moses. "You know the camping places. You know the way through this wilderness, where there is no path. Be our guide! Please come with us, and we'll share with you everything the Lord gives us."

Jethro said good-bye and went back to his own family and his own country. But some of his relatives, the Kenites, went along with the Israelites.

Then the Lord told Moses, "Make two silver trumpets and give them to Aaron's sons to call the people together. Use them in Canaan to sound the signal for battle."

Aaron's sons blew the trumpets, and the people folded up their tents and got ready to move out across the vast and terrible wilderness to the land of Canaan.

First the priests carefully took down God's tent. They wrapped the tabernacle and the furniture up in leather and blue cloth for the Levites to carry as they marched along.

The Israelites marched and camped in a special order, given to Moses by God. The ark of the covenant was always located in the middle of the people.

Each time they made camp, the Israelites first set up the tabernacle, with the courtyard around it and the altar in front of it. Then the people set up their own tents around God's tent in groups of families and tribes. Moses and Aaron and their families camped right in front of the tabernacle, and the other Levites camped on the other three sides.

Further out from the tabernacle were the tents of the other twelve tribes. Three tribes camped on each of the four sides, all of them facing the tabernacle. Each tribe flew its own banner beside its camping place.

The Israelites left Mount Sinai in the spring on the twentieth day of the fourteenth month after they escaped from Egypt. They traveled by stages across the wilderness, stopping many times to make camp.

As they marched, they followed the pillar of cloud by day and the pillar of fire by night. They stayed wherever the cloud stayed, sometimes for a few days, sometimes for a month, sometimes for a year. They stayed in camp as long as the cloud stayed over the tabernacle, but when the cloud lifted, they set out for a new place. The Lord was their guide through the wilderness.

21

The Graves of Greed

Numbers 11—12

THREE days after they left Mount Sinai, the Israelites began to complain. When the Lord heard them, he was so angry he sent fire to burn among them. The hot flames completely destroyed one end of the camp.

The people cried out in fear to Moses. He prayed to the Lord for them, and the fire died out. They named that place Taberah, which means "burning," because of the fire.

After they left Taberah, the complaining began again. Traveling along with the Israelites were some other people who had come with them from Egypt. These people wanted meat, and they encouraged the Israelites to complain.

"Oh, if we could just have some meat to eat!" they cried. "Remember how we ate all the fish we wanted in Egypt! Remember the cucumbers and melons, the leeks and the onions and the garlic! But now we're hungry, and there's nothing to eat but this same old manna day after day. We're tired of it!"

Manna was the bread from heaven that God gave them every morning except the sabbath. When they cooked it, it tasted like honey cakes, but after all these months they wanted something more.

The people stood around in front of their tents talking, and Moses heard their complaints. Moses was unhappy because the complaints were making the Lord angry.

"Why have you been so hard on me, your servant?" Moses asked the Lord. "What have I done to displease you? Why did you put me in charge of all these people anyway? Am I their mother? Are they my babies to feed and carry to Canaan? They pester me with their complaints for meat. Where can I find enough meat for so many people? Oh, have mercy, Lord, and kill me, so my troubles will be over!"

"I'll help you," answered the Lord. "Tell the people to get ready. Tomorrow I'll send them meat. Tell them I've heard their complaints. I'll give them so much meat they'll eat it not just for one day, or two days, or five days, or ten days, or twenty days, but for a whole month—until it comes out their noses and makes them sick! They've rejected me, even though I live right here in the middle of them. They whine and say they were better off in Egypt."

Moses answered, "There are too many people, Lord! There are more than the stars in the sky! And you say you'll give them enough meat for a whole month! Where would we get enough sheep and cattle for so many people to eat for so long? If all the fish in the sea were caught, it wouldn't be enough to feed them!"

"Is there any limit to my power?" asked the Lord. "You'll see today whether I can do what I say!"

Then the Lord sent a wind which brought an enormous flock of small, fat birds into the camp. They were quails, flying in from the Great Western Sea. They rested on the ground in and around the camp for miles in every direction. There were so many that when they landed they piled up three feet deep on the ground! God rained down meat on the people like dust, and the birds were as thick as the sand on the seashore.

All that day, all that night, and all the next day the people were busy catching quails. Everyone caught at least fifty bushels of them. They killed them and spread them out to dry. Soon they were roasting the meat and feasting on it.

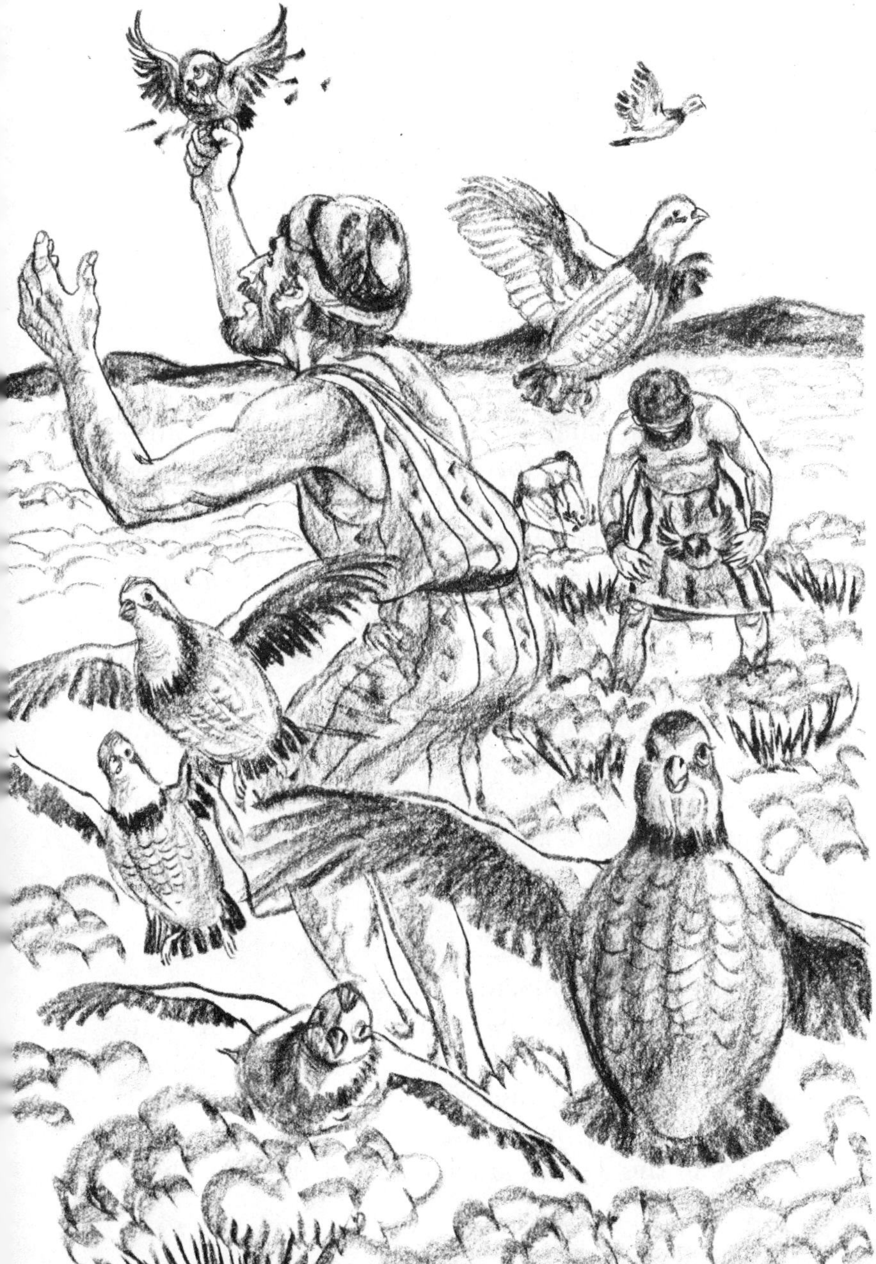

But while the meat was still between their teeth, the Lord struck them with a terrible sickness. In his anger he caused many of them to die.

They named that place "Graves of Greed," because there they dug graves to bury the greedy people who died because they were not satisfied with what God gave them.

From the Graves of Greed they went on to Hazeroth, where another disaster struck.

This time the complaints came from Miriam and Aaron. They criticized their brother Moses for marrying a foreigner, because they were jealous of his leadership.

"Is Moses the only one the Lord has spoken to?" they complained. "Hasn't he spoken through us as well?"

Moses was so humble he said nothing, but the Lord was annoyed.

"Moses, Aaron, and Miriam!" he called. "Come to the tabernacle, you three!"

As they arrived at the tabernacle, the Lord came down in a pillar of cloud and stood at the entrance of the tent calling, "Aaron! Miriam!"

They both stepped forward.

"Now listen to me!" said the Lord. "I speak to prophets in dreams, and I show myself to them in visions. But Moses is more than a prophet. With him I speak directly, and I've shown him my glory. I have put Moses in charge of my people. How dare you speak against my servant Moses!"

Then the Lord's anger blazed against them,

and the cloud left the tent. The two brothers were shocked to see Miriam's skin turn as white as snow. They knew she had leprosy, a dreaded disease.

"Please, sir!" cried Aaron to Moses. "Don't punish us for our foolishness and our sin! Don't let her become like a dead person, with half her body eaten away by disease!"

So Moses prayed, "Please, not this, Lord! Heal her, I pray!"

The Lord answered, "If her father had spit in her face, she would have to hide in shame for seven days. She has offended me. Send her out of the camp for seven days, and then let her come back."

So Moses' prayer was answered, and Miriam was healed, but she had to stay outside the camp for seven days as punishment.

22

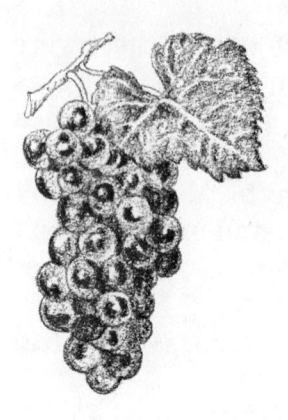

The Spies Who Were Afraid of Giants

Numbers 13—14

IT was midsummer in Canaan, the season of the first ripe grapes. In the desert to the south, the Israelites were preparing to enter the land. They were camped at an oasis called Kadesh-barnea, near the border of the land of Canaan.

The Lord told Moses to send spies into Canaan, because the Israelites would need information about the land before they left the wilderness.

Moses chose twelve men, one leader from each tribe, and he gave them these orders:

"Go by way of the desert of southern Canaan,

and then into the hill country. Find out what the land is like, whether it's good or poor for planting, and whether forests grow there. Do your best to bring back some of the fruit. See whether the cities are open or surrounded by strong walls. Find out how many people live there and whether they're weak or powerful."

The twelve spies set out to explore the land of Canaan. They crossed the desert of southern Canaan and entered the ancient city of Hebron, where tall people called Anaks lived.

They explored the land from the wilderness in the south to the mountains in the north.

When they reached the valley of Eshcol, they found some ripe grapes, and they cut a branch with a single bunch of fruit. It was so heavy that it took two men to carry the bunch of grapes on a pole! They also picked some figs and pomegranates.

After forty days of exploring, the twelve spies returned to Kadesh-barnea.

"We explored the land from one end to the other," they reported. "We found that the people who live there are very strong. Their cities are large and well-defended, with walls that reach the sky! What's worse, we saw the Anaks, and they're huge! We saw other powerful people—the Amalekites, who live in the south; the Hittites, the Jebusites, and the Amorites, who live in the hill country; and the Canaanites, who live by the sea and alongside the River Jordan."

Then one of the spies, a man named Caleb, interrupted the others. "Quiet! Let's stop this kind of talk. Look at this fruit. Have you ever seen such a bunch of grapes? Canaan is truly rich and fertile, a land of milk and honey, as the Lord said. We should go up there right now and take the land. We're strong enough to do it!"

"No! No!" cried all the others except Joshua. "We can't attack those people. We're not strong enough. They're too much for us!"

They frightened the people with their discouraging report. "The land is terrible!" they said. "And the people we saw were enormous. We saw giants! When we looked at them, we felt like grasshoppers, and that's probably what we looked like to them!"

That night the people stayed up talking about the bad report of the ten frightened spies. They ignored the good report of Caleb and Joshua. They forgot that the Lord would go on ahead of them. They forgot that the Lord would fight for them. They were afraid, and they cried and grumbled and complained.

"Oh, if only we had died in Egypt, or in the wilderness," some said. "Why is the Lord taking us into such a terrible place? We'll all be killed in battle, and our wives and children will be taken prisoners. It would be better if we just went back to Egypt."

"The Lord hates us," cried some others. "He has brought us out of Egypt so our enemies can destroy us!"

Then they began to complain about Moses and Aaron. They were thinking about choosing someone else to lead them.

"We'll go back to Egypt without them," they whispered.

When Moses and Aaron found out what the people were saying, they came and bowed down in prayer in front of all the people.

Caleb and Joshua joined them, and they were

so sad that they tore their clothes in mourning, as if someone had died.

"The land we saw is a wonderful place," they told the people. "If the Lord is pleased with us, he'll take us there and give it to us. Don't be afraid of the people who live there. We'll easily defeat them. They have no protection, and we have the Lord with us. He'll fight for us. He'll help us as he did in Egypt and in the wilderness. Don't rebel against the Lord!"

But the people answered by picking up stones and rocks to throw at them. They would have stoned Caleb and Joshua to death, but suddenly the glory of the Lord appeared like a bright light over the tabernacle. The people saw it and they dropped their stones.

Then the Lord said to Moses, "How much longer will these people refuse to trust me? After all I've done for them, after all the signs I've shown them, they still treat me without respect. I'll strike them dead to keep them from the land of Canaan!"

"Please, Lord," prayed Moses. "These are the people you brought out of Egypt! What will the Egyptians think if you destroy your people? And the nations around here have heard of you. They know you're with us and guiding us. If you kill your people here in the wilderness, they'll say you weren't able to give them the land as you promised. Please be patient with your people, Lord. Please forgive their sin! You said you're slow to anger, faithful and loving, forgiving and merciful, and, Lord, you've forgiven so much already."

"All right, Moses. I'll answer your prayer. I won't kill them. But none of these men and women will see the land which I have promised. Ten times they've tested me and disobeyed me. Only Caleb and Joshua have loved me. Because of this, I'll bring them and their families into the land of Canaan. But none of the others will ever see it. Tomorrow you must all leave Kadesh and return to the wilderness!

"Tell the people, 'You will wander in the wilderness for forty years—one year for each day that the spies explored the land. You will die in the wilderness as you feared, because you didn't trust me. After all the grown-ups have died, your children will enter the Promised Land. They will enjoy what you have rejected. You will suffer for your sins by wandering for forty years, and after all the fathers and mothers are dead their children will enter Canaan.'"

Then the ten spies who gave the bad report were all struck dead.

When the people saw this, and when they heard what God had said, they were sorry and they began to cry.

Early the next morning they got up and said, "Look! Let's go to Canaan! Why should we wait forty years? We're ready to enter now! We sinned yesterday, it's true, but now we're not afraid.

We'll enter the land the Lord has told us about! We're on our way!"

But it was too late.

"Don't disobey the Lord," Moses warned. "The Lord isn't with you now. You can't succeed. The Amalekites and the Canaanites will defeat you in battle."

But the people fastened on their weapons and went out, up into the hill country, even though the Lord wasn't with them. They ran out like a mob, confused and without leaders.

The Amalekites and the Canaanites came down from their homes in the hill country and attacked the Israelites. They chased them like bees all the way out of the land, and many of the Israelites were killed.

The rest of them returned weeping and wailing to the wilderness, for without the Lord fighting for them, they could not win.

23

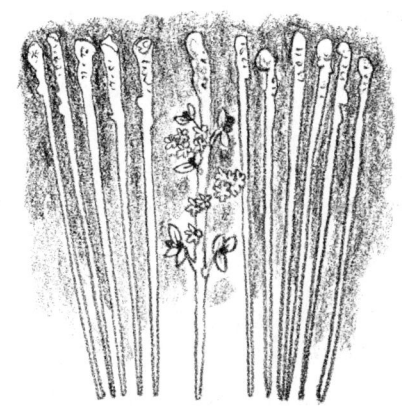

Angry Rebels and Aaron's Rod

Numbers 16—17

THE Lord wanted the Israelites to be his people, but they kept disobeying his instructions. They rebelled against him and his servant, Moses.

One of Moses' cousins, a Levite named Korah, wasn't satisfied with his job of helping the priests in the tabernacle. He wanted to be a priest himself. Korah talked two hundred and fifty other Levites into going with him to complain to Moses and Aaron.

"We've had enough of you!" Korah said to

them. "You're no better than the rest of us! Why are you setting yourselves up over the Lord's people? We're just as good as you are!"

When Moses heard Korah's complaint, he fell on the ground to pray. Then he got up and told the rebels, "Tomorrow the Lord will show whom he has chosen for priests. Come to the tabernacle, all of you, and bring fire pans with you. Put fire and incense in the pans and bring them to the altar. The Lord will show who will be allowed to bring offerings to him. He chose you to serve in the tabernacle, but you want to act as priests. You've gone too far, you Levites!"

The next day Korah and all his men met Moses and Aaron at the entrance of the tabernacle. The two hundred and fifty men with him presented incense to the Lord, and so did Aaron.

Suddenly the glory of the Lord appeared as a bright light before all the people.

"Stand back!" warned the Lord. "Moses and Aaron, get away from these men, and I'll destroy them right now!"

Then the Lord sent a fire that burned up Korah and all his men.

Some others were causing trouble, also. Two men named Dathan and Abiram refused to appear when Moses sent for them.

"We won't come," they said. "You've brought us from the wonderful land of Egypt to this awful wilderness to kill us, and now you want to boss us around! Where's the rich and fertile land you promised us? Where are our fields and vineyards? You can't trick us anymore! We're not coming!"

Moses went with the leaders of the people to the tents of Dathan and Abiram.

"Get back!" he warned the others. "Move away from the tents of these wicked men, and don't touch any of their belongings, or you'll be destroyed!"

The people backed away.

Dathan and Abiram came out of their tents and stood at the entrances with their wives and children.

"You'll know the Lord sent me, and it wasn't my idea to lead you," said Moses to the people. "If these men die a natural death, then the Lord didn't send me. But if the Lord opens the ground into a great pit and it swallows them alive, then you'll know that these men are rebels!"

Just as Moses finished speaking, the ground under Dathan and Abiram split wide open, and the earth swallowed them alive, along with their wives and children and tents and belongings. They screamed, and then, as the earth closed up over them, they disappeared.

The people standing by Moses saw them disappear and they heard the screams. They were so scared they ran away, shouting, "Hurry, get away, or the earth will swallow us, too!"

They were too frightened that day to say or do anything else, but the next day they were complaining about Moses and Aaron again. "You've killed the Lord's people!" they said.

But as they got near the tents of Moses and Aaron, they saw the cloud covering the tabernacle, and the glory of the Lord appeared, shining like a bright light.

Moses and Aaron came out to meet the people who were complaining about them.

"Stand back!" the Lord warned them. "I'm going to destroy these rebels right now!"

Moses and Aaron quickly bowed down with their faces to the ground.

"Quick!" Moses told Aaron. "Take your fire pan and put incense on it. Hurry and go to the people, to take away their guilt. Hurry, for I feel the Lord's anger coming against them already! A sickness has started to break out among the people."

Aaron rushed to the middle of the camp with his fire pan. He found the people already sick, and some were dying. He put incense in the fire pan and offered it to the Lord, to ask forgiveness for the people. He made the sacrifice right there, between the living and the dead. God accepted the sacrifice, and the sickness stopped.

The angry rebels had brought death to themselves and many Israelites.

Soon after this, the Lord said to Moses, "Tell the Israelites to give you a rod for each tribe. Tell the leader of each tribe to write his name on his rod, and tell Aaron to write his name on the rod of the tribe of Levi. Take all the rods and put them in the tabernacle, in front of the ark of the covenant. The rod of the man I choose to be my priest will sprout like a live branch. And that will put a stop to this complaining about who leads my people!"

The chief of each tribe brought a rod, and all the rods were put with Aaron's rod in the tabernacle in front of the ark.

The next day Moses went inside the tabernacle

and found that one rod had sprouted like a live branch. Ripe almonds and pale pink blossoms were growing from Aaron's rod!

He brought all the rods out to show the people, and the chiefs of each tribe took back their dead rods. Moses kept Aaron's rod, which was a live branch.

"Put Aaron's rod back in front of the Ark," the Lord told Moses. "It will be a warning to the rebels, to keep them from sinning."

24

Moses Disobeys God

Numbers 20

For many years the Israelites wandered from place to place, camping in the wilderness. As time passed, many of the older people died, and their bodies were scattered in the desert.

One year they came again to Kadesh-barnea, the oasis on the border between the wilderness and the land of Canaan. While they were camped there, Miriam died and Moses and Aaron disobeyed God.

That year there was no water at Kadesh, and the people complained to Moses and Aaron.

"We wish we were dead!" they cried. "We wish the Lord had burned us up along with Korah! We wish he had let us be swallowed up in the pit with Dathan and Abiram! Why did you bring us into this wilderness to die? Why did you bring us out of Egypt to this miserable desert, where nothing can live? No grain or figs, grapes or pomegranates grow in this awful place, and there isn't even any water to drink!"

Moses and Aaron went to the entrance of the tabernacle and bowed down to pray.

The glory of the Lord appeared to them, and the Lord said to Moses, "Take Aaron's rod and go to that large rock. Then, right in front of all the people, speak to the rock, and water will flow out of it for the people and their animals to drink."

Moses took the rod from its place in front of the ark, and he and Aaron called the people to come and stand in front of the rock.

Moses shouted at the people, "Listen to me, you rebels!"

He raised his hand. "Must we get water out of this rock for you?"

Then he struck the rock twice with the rod.

Water gushed out of the rock and poured onto the ground. The thirsty people and animals came to drink.

But Moses had disobeyed the Lord.

"You didn't trust me," the Lord said to Moses and Aaron. "You didn't follow my directions. You didn't honor me in front of the people. Because of this, I'm not going to let you lead the people into the Promised Land."

That place was called Meribah, which means "argument," because the people argued with the Lord. And because of what happened at Meribah, Moses and Aaron never reached the land of Canaan.

When the people finished drinking, the Lord told Moses it was time to leave Kadesh-barnea. The forty years of wandering were nearly over.

Moses sent messengers to the king of Edom to ask permission to pass through his land.

The Israelite messengers told the king, "We've had a hard time in Egypt, and the Lord rescued us. Now we're camped at Kadesh-barnea, at the edge of your territory. Please let us pass through. Remember, we're your relatives. Your ancestor, Esau, was the twin brother of our ancestor, Jacob. If we pass through your land we won't hurt your fields and vineyards or drink water from your wells. We'll stay on the king's highway and we won't go off the main road until we're through your territory."

The king's highway was a caravan track, an important trade route between Egypt and Syria, which passed through Edom.

But the king of Edom refused to let them pass. "You may not go through our land," he said. "If you try, we'll attack you!"

"But we'll stay on the main road," begged the Israelites. "If we or our animals drink any of your water, we'll pay for it. Just let us walk through—it's such a small thing to ask!"

"No. Go away," he said.

Then the king of Edom called out his large, powerful army, and the Israelites turned away to avoid battle. Instead of going on the king's highway, they traveled up the valley called the Arabah, from Kadesh to the border of Edom.

When they arrived at Mount Hor, the Lord said to Moses and Aaron, "You two must die without entering the Promised Land, because you both rebelled against me at Meribah. It's time for Aaron to die now. Take him and his son Eleazar up to the top of Mount Hor. Take Aaron's priestly clothes and put them on his son, for

Eleazar will be high priest after Aaron."

The people watched as the three men walked away toward Mount Hor.

When they got to the top of the mountain, Moses put Aaron's priestly clothes on Eleazar. Then Moses and Eleazar walked down from the mountain without Aaron, and Aaron died alone on the mountaintop.

When the Israelites heard that Aaron was dead, they mourned for him for thirty days.

25

God Fights the Canaanite Kings

Numbers 21

WHEN the people finished mourning for Aaron, they left Mount Hor and began the march around Edom.

On the way they again lost faith and began to complain against the Lord and his servant, Moses.

"Why have you brought us out of Egypt to die in this wilderness?" they cried. "We have nothing to eat but this awful manna!"

The Lord was angry again. This time he sent poisonous snakes to punish the people.

"We've sinned!" cried the people. "Please, Moses, pray to the Lord to take away these snakes!"

Moses prayed for them, and the Lord answered.

"Make a bronze snake," he told Moses, "and put it up on a pole like a flag. Tell everyone who has been bitten by the poisonous snakes to look at the bronze snake, and they'll get well."

So Moses made the bronze snake and put it on a pole, and the people who were bitten by poisonous snakes looked up and lived.

When everyone was well, the Israelites moved on past Edom. They crossed the Arnon River, moved down into the valley of Moab, and set up camp on the border between the land of the Moabites and the land of the Amorites.

The Lord planned to give the Israelites the land that belonged to the Canaanites and the Amorites. He didn't give them the land of the Edomites, the Moabites, or the Ammonites, because those nations were related to the Israelites.

From their camp on the edge of the land of the Amorites, the Israelites sent messengers to Sihon, a king of the Amorites.

"Let us pass through your kingdom," they said. "We won't go into your fields or vineyards, and we won't drink water from your wells. We'll stay on the main road until we pass through your territory."

But Sihon refused to let the Israelites go through his country. Instead, he called out his army to attack them.

"Don't worry," said the Lord. "I've put Sihon and his kingdom into your hands. Go in. Today I'll begin to make all the nations afraid of you."

When Sihon and his army attacked, the Israelites met them and defeated them, killing King Sihon in battle.

After the battle, the Israelites took all of Sihon's land from the Arnon River to the Jabbok River. They captured many Amorite cities and towns, including Sihon's capital, and they drove out the people who lived there.

Next the Israelites moved up the road to Bashan, a small kingdom north of the Jabbok River. Og, the king of Bashan, marched out with his army to fight them. Og was a giant, famous for his size.

"Don't be afraid of Og," the Lord told Moses, "for I'm handing him over to you, along with his people and his land. I'm putting them into your power, so you'll defeat them as you defeated Sihon."

The Israelites met Og and his army, and they fought on foot with bows, slings, stones, and spears. They killed all of Og's men and took his land.

Now the Israelites were in control of all the land on the east side of the Jordan, from the Arnon River to Mount Hermon. With the Lord fighting for them, they could not lose.

26

Balaam and His Blessings

Numbers 22—24

THE Israelites were camped in the valley of Moab, across the Jordan River from Jericho. They controlled all the land north of the Arnon River and east of the Jordan.

South of the Arnon lived the Moabites, who were feeling sick because they were so afraid of the Israelites.

When they heard the news of the Israelite victories over Sihon and Og, they went to their neighbors, the Midianites. They told the Midianites, "This mob of Israelites will chew up all the pasture grass around us. They're like an ox in a spring field."

Balak, the king of Moab, was afraid to fight the Israelites with his army, because there were so many of them. He decided to try something else.

Far to the north of Moab, near the Euphrates River, lived a famous magician and fortune-teller named Balaam. Perhaps, thought Balak, magic would work where weapons had failed. Perhaps Balaam could help defeat the Israelites.

Balak sent messengers to Balaam. When they arrived at his home, they said, "A whole nation has come out of Egypt, and they cover the face of the land. They're spreading everywhere! Right now they're camped at my doorstep, threatening to take my land! Come at once and curse them, for they're too powerful for me! Perhaps with your help I can defeat them and drive them out of our land. I know that whomever you bless stays blessed, and whomever you curse stays cursed."

The messengers offered silver and gold to bribe Balaam to use his powers against Israel.

"Stay here tonight," Balaam told them, "and tomorrow I'll report to you whatever God tells me."

That night God asked Balaam, "Who are these men and what are they doing here?"

"They're messengers from Balak, king of Moab. He wants me to curse some people who have come out of Egypt to take over his land. He wants me to get rid of them."

"Don't go with these men," said God. "You must not curse these people, for I have given them my blessing."

The next morning Balaam went to the messengers and said, "Go home, for the Lord won't let me go with you."

Balak's men went back to Moab and told the king that Balaam was refusing their offer. So Balak sent a larger number of more important messengers.

"Balak asks you to come to him no matter what," these men said to Balaam. "He'll give you a great reward—whatever you ask—if you'll just come and curse these people for him."

Still Balaam refused.

"Even if Balak gave me all the silver and gold in his palace," he said, "I wouldn't disobey God. But stay here tonight. I'll ask again."

That night God told Balaam, "If these men ask you to go, then go, but do only what I tell you to do."

God was not pleased that Balaam wanted to go with the Moabites. He knew that Balaam wanted the reward.

The next morning Balaam got up and saddled his donkey and went back to Moab with Balak's messengers.

But God was angry at Balaam, and as he rode on his donkey with his two servants walking beside him, the angel of the Lord blocked his way on the road.

The men didn't see the angel, but the donkey did. The angel was holding out a sword and looking so fierce that the donkey was frightened and it turned off the road and went into a field.

Balaam beat the donkey to bring it back onto the road.

Then the angel stood at a place where the road ran between two vineyards, with stone walls on each side.

When the donkey saw the angel again, it pressed against the wall, crushing Balaam's foot.

He beat the animal again.

Then the angel moved on further down the

road and stood at a place where there was no room to turn right or left.

When the donkey saw the angel this time, it just lay down on the road and refused to move at all.

Then Balaam lost his temper and beat the donkey hard with his stick.

The Lord let the donkey speak, and it said, "What have I done? Why have you beaten me three times?"

"You've been making a fool of me!" shouted Balaam. "If I had a sword in my hand, I'd kill you right here and now!"

"But I'm your donkey, the same one you've ridden all your life. Have I ever done anything like this to you before?"

"No, you haven't."

Then the Lord let Balaam see the angel standing on the road in front of him, with his sword in his hand. Balaam bowed down in front of him.

"Why have you beaten your donkey three times?" asked the angel. "I came to block your way, but you headed straight for me. Three times your donkey saw me and three times it turned away. Otherwise, I would have killed you."

"I've done wrong!" cried Balaam. "I didn't know you were standing on the road to block me. If you don't want me to go on, I'll return home."

"Go on now," said the angel. "Go with these men, but say only what I tell you to say."

So Balaam continued on his way to Moab.

Balak came out to meet him by the river Arnon, at the border of Moab.

"What took you so long?" he demanded. "Why didn't you come the first time I sent for you? Did you think I couldn't pay you?"

"Look, here I am," answered Balaam. "I have no power to tell you anything. I can speak only the words that God puts into my mouth."

The next morning Balak took him to a high place where they could look out and see the Israelite camp.

"Build me seven altars and bring me seven bulls and seven rams," said Balaam.

Balak did as he was asked, and he offered a bull and a ram on each altar.

Balaam looked for magic signs in the offerings, to help him with his fortune-telling, and then he said, "Stay here and I'll go off by myself to find out if the Lord has a message for me."

In a little while Balaam returned to Balak, who was standing beside the altars with the Moabite leaders.

Then Balaam gave the message from the Lord:

> Balak, king of Moab, has brought me here to curse the Israelites.
> But I can't curse those whom God has not cursed.
> I see the Israelites living apart, different from other nations.
> They are so numerous, nobody can count them.
> May I live a good life and die in peace,
> As the Israelites are sure to do!

"What have you done to me!" cried Balak. "I brought you here to curse my enemies, and you have blessed them!"

"What can I do?" asked Balaam. "The Lord puts the words in my mouth."

"Then let's go somewhere else," said Balak. "Let's go where you can see more of them. Curse them for me there."

He took Balaam to a field on the top of Mount Pisgah. There he built seven more altars and sacrificed a bull and a ram on each one.

Balaam examined the offerings for more magic signs. Then he said, "Stay here while I go off alone."

After a while he came back and found Balak standing beside the altars with the Moabite leaders.

"What does the Lord say now?" asked Balak.

Balaam gave the second message:

>Come, Balak, and listen to me!
>God is not like a human being, who tells lies and changes his mind.
>When God says something, he does it!
>God has told me to bless the Israelites, and I must obey!
>The Lord their God is with them.
>He is their king.
>No magic spells can work against them.
>People will look at Israel and say,
>"Look what God has done!"
>Israel is rearing up like a lion!
>He won't lie down again until he eats up his enemies!

Balak was furious.

"If you can't curse them, then don't bless them," he shouted. "Don't say anything at all!"

"I warned you," said Balaam. "I told you I must do whatever the Lord tells me to do."

"Come, let's try again," said Balak. "Let's go to another place. Perhaps God will let you curse them if we go somewhere else."

He took Balaam to the top of Mount Peor, overlooking the desert. He built seven more altars and offered seven bulls and seven rams.

By now Balaam realized that the Lord wanted him to bless Israel, so this time he didn't look at the offerings for magic signs. Instead, he turned toward the desert, where he could see the Israelites camped tribe by tribe.

Then the spirit of God came upon Balaam, and he said:

> How fine are your tents, O Israel!
> Like long rows of palm trees,
> Like gardens beside a river!
> The king of Israel will be greater than all kings!
> Their kingdom will be lifted up.
> God brought them out of Egypt,
> And he is fighting for them like a wild ox.
> He will destroy their enemies.
> He'll eat them up and crunch their bones!
> Whoever blesses them will be blessed,
> And whoever curses them will be cursed.

When he heard this, Balak was so angry he shook his clenched fists at Balaam and screamed,

"I brought you here to curse my enemies, and you've blessed them three times. Get out of here! Go back where you came from! I was going to give you a great reward, but the Lord has kept it from you!"

"I told you from the beginning that I would obey the Lord," answered Balaam. "If you gave me all the silver and gold in your palace, I would still say what the Lord told me to say. I'll go home right away. But before I leave, let me warn you what the Israelites are going to do."

Then Balaam gave his last message:

> I look far into the future, and this is what I see:
> A star, a king, rises like a comet from Israel.
> He strikes Moab and conquers Edom;
> He tramples down all his enemies.

Then Balaam got up and left. Balak's plan had failed.

27

Don't Worship Idols!

Numbers 25—26, 31—34

WHEN Balak's plan for defeating the Israelites with curses failed, the Moabites tried something else. This time they almost succeeded.

Balaam, the magician, changed his mind about going home. He wanted Balak's silver and gold, so he gave the king some advice.

The Moabites and their neighbors, the Midianites, worshiped an idol called the Baal of Peor. At Balaam's suggestion, the women of Moab came to the Israelite camp and invited the men to join them in worshiping their idol. Balaam knew that this would make the Lord very angry, and he hoped that the Lord would destroy the Israelites.

When the Lord saw his people bowing down to Baal, he said to Moses, "Take all the idol worshipers and kill them. Punish them right now, in broad daylight, and then I'll forgive the people."

Moses told the leaders of the tribes to put to death the men who had gone to worship the idol.

After the idol worshipers were killed, the Lord told Moses, "Now go and attack the Midianites for hurting Israel with their sly tricks."

Moses told the people, "Choose the best fighting men to go to war against the Midianites, to punish them. Pick a fighting unit from each tribe."

Twelve units of fighting men came, and Moses sent them out with Phineas, the son of Eleazar the high priest. Eleazar blew the trumpets to signal the start of the battle.

The Israelite army attacked the Midianites and killed all the men, including five kings and Balaam the magician. They captured the women, children, and all their belongings. They burned the Midianite cities and army camps and came back to Moses with the captives and the loot.

Moses and Eleazar came out to meet the army. They saw the Israelite soldiers with their arms full of gold, silver, bronze, iron, tin, lead, and bracelets, rings, earrings, and necklaces. But when Moses saw the Midianite prisoners, he was very angry.

"Why did you take prisoners?" he asked. "Why did you let these women live? These are the same women who led the Israelites to worship the idol at Peor! It's their fault that so many Israelites died!"

He let them keep just the young girls, who became their brides.

Then Moses counted the loot and divided it among the soldiers and the rest of the people. He gave some to the priests and the Levites, too.

By now all the people who were counted at Sinai were dead, except Moses, Caleb, and Joshua. Their children were grown-ups, with children of their own. The Lord told Moses to count the people again, so they could divide the land of Canaan fairly.

Moses and the leaders counted the people, and the Lord told Moses how to divide the land. They would cross the Jordan River and capture the land on the west bank. More land would be given to the larger tribes and less to the smaller tribes. The Levites would have no land of their own.

Some men from the tribes of Reuben and Gad came to Moses with a special request. They thought the land on the east side of the Jordan River would be a nice place to stay. It was good grazing land, and they owned a large number of animals.

"Please let us have this land," they asked. "Don't make us go with you across the Jordan. We like it here."

"That's not fair to the others," said Moses. "Why should you stay here where we've already conquered the land and let them fight on the west side without you? You must go with us."

"Then please let us build pens for our sheep and homes for our families," they said. "We'll cross the Jordan with the others and help them conquer the land, but please let us come back here to settle."

Finally Moses agreed. "The Lord will drive our enemies away," he said. "He'll conquer the land for us. Then you may come back here and settle."

Moses made a list of all the camping places the Israelites had made on their long journey from Egypt. Between Rameses in Egypt and the plains of Moab they had camped at forty different sites.

The Lord told Moses that the land of Canaan would be theirs from the desert in the south to the mountains in the north and from the Great Western Sea to the wilderness in the east. He would fight for them and give them the land.

28

Remembering God's Teaching

Deuteronomy 1—11

THE Israelites were almost ready to enter the Promised Land. They were camped on the east side of the Jordan River, on the edge of the wilderness.

Before they crossed the river, Moses spoke to them, reminding them of everything the Lord had done for them. He told them the story of how God had led his people through the wilderness from Sinai, a journey that had taken them almost forty years.

"The Lord carried you here as a father carries

his child," said Moses. He told them how God had rescued their parents from Egypt, and given them the Ten Commandments and other laws at Mount Sinai. He told them how God wanted them to live, and he reminded them of God's instructions.

God always kept his promises, said Moses. He was faithful. They could trust him. He rescued them from slavery, he took care of them in the wilderness, and he would defeat their enemies in the land of Canaan.

"Pay attention to God's teaching," said Moses. "If you do, you'll enjoy the land the Lord is giving to you. If you obey him, people of other nations will notice. No other people on earth has a great God like the Lord. He is near us when we need him, and he answers us when we call on him for help."

Most of the people were too young to remember Egypt or Sinai, and they listened eagerly as Moses repeated the story and explained God's teaching.

"Listen, people of Israel! The Lord our God is the one and only God! Love the Lord your God with all your mind and all your heart and all your strength! Write my words on your heart. Remember God's instructions and teach them to your children and grandchildren. Speak to your children about the Lord when you're at home and when you're traveling away from home. Teach your children about the Lord when you get up in the morning, during the day, and when you put them to bed at night.

"Remember how the Lord led you on this long journey through the wilderness. For forty years he was teaching you to obey him. He let you go hungry, then he gave you manna to teach you to trust him. He took such good care of you that your clothes didn't wear out, and your sandals lasted for forty years!

"If you obey the Lord, he'll give you everything you need. He'll bring you into the land and give you great cities which you didn't build, houses full of things you didn't buy, wells you didn't dig, and gardens you didn't plant. Don't forget him. Don't worship idols.

"The Lord chose you from all the peoples in the world to be his own special people. He didn't do this because you're the greatest or the best. You're not. He chose you because he loves you. If you obey him, he'll keep his promises and bless you.

"He is God of heaven and earth, God of gods and Lord of lords, the great, mighty, and terrible God. If you remember his teaching, he'll raise you high above all other nations so you can bring him praise and glory and be his holy people."

29

Choose Life!

Deuteronomy 27—34

MOSES was telling the Israelites what to do when they entered the Promised Land.

"On the day you cross the Jordan River, set up some stones with my laws and teachings on them. Use the stones as an altar to the Lord your God.

"During the long years in the wilderness, God has prepared your hearts to understand his ways. He was teaching you how to live in the Promised Land. Now you are ready.

"God's teaching isn't too hard to obey. It's not beyond your reach. It's not up in the sky. You don't have to go up and bring it down. It's not on the other side of the ocean. You don't have to cross the sea. No, God's Word is here with you. It's in your mouth and in your heart. You know it and you can say it, so you can obey it!

"Today," said Moses, "I'm giving you a choice between good and evil, between life and death. If you obey the Lord, he'll give you many blessings, and you'll become a great nation. If you disobey him, if you worship idols, you'll suffer and be destroyed. You have a choice today between God's blessing and his curse, between life and death. Choose life!"

Then Moses wrote down all God's instructions and gave them to the Levites to put with the ark of the covenant. He told the Levites to read all of God's Word to the people every seven years, to help them obey the Lord.

"I'm an old man," he said. "I'm a hundred and twenty years old today, too old to lead you. The Lord has told me that I can't cross the Jordan with you. But don't be afraid. The Lord your God will lead you. He'll destroy your enemies and give you the land. He'll be with you."

Then Moses called Joshua and he laid his hands on Joshua's head. "The Lord has chosen Joshua to guide you to the Promised Land," said Moses. "You won't be like sheep without a shepherd. God's spirit is in Joshua."

Then Moses said to Joshua, "Be strong. Be brave. You have been chosen to bring the Israelites into the Promised Land. The Lord himself will lead you, and he'll fight for you. He won't fail you or leave you. He'll be with you. Don't be afraid."

The Lord gave Moses a last message for the people. It was a song, and Moses taught it to the Israelites before he died.

> Listen, O heaven and earth!
> Great is our God, the Creator of perfect work.
> I'll praise the name of the Lord,
> And his people will tell of his glory!
> The Lord chose his people and he takes care of them.
> The Lord is like an eagle, teaching his babies to fly.
> He pushes them out of the nest,
> Then he catches them safely on his outstretched wings.
> He feeds them and cares for them.
> He keeps them from falling.
> Truly, he loves his people!

Then the Lord said to Moses, "Go up to the top of Mount Nebo. From there you can look out over the land of Canaan. And there you'll die, like your brother Aaron, because you disobeyed me at Meribah. But before you die I'll show you the Promised Land."

Then Moses blessed the people, tribe by tribe, and said farewell. "Remember, the words of the Lord are your life," he said. Then for the last time the old man walked away from the Israelite camp. He walked slowly toward Mount Nebo and climbed the mountain all alone.

At the top of the mountain the Lord showed

Moses all the land of Canaan, from the shore of the Great Western Sea to the hill country and the fertile river valleys, from the snow-covered mountains to the sandy deserts.

Moses died there in the land of Moab. The Lord buried Moses in a place nobody has ever found.

The Israelites mourned their leader for thirty days. They never forgot him. When they got to the Promised Land, they remembered the teachings of Moses, the servant of God.

Eve Bowers MacMaster is writing the Story Bible Series because she wants to share her love for the Bible with others. Several years ago she was looking for a story Bible to read to her three young children, and not finding what she wanted, she decided to write one herself.

Book 1 in the series is *God's Family*, all the stories from Genesis, the first book of the Bible. This is the second. The other volumes are in process.

Eve has taught in the Bible department at Eastern Mennonite College and in the history department at James Madison University, both located in Harrisonburg, Virginia.

She has degrees in history from George Washington University and Pennsylvania State University. She taught English as a foreign language while serving as a Peace Corps Volunteer in Turkey. While living and working in the Middle East, she visited many of the places mentioned in the Bible.

Eve is married to Richard MacMaster, a writer, teacher, and historian. They live with their three children, Sam, Tom, and Sarah, in Bridgewater, Virginia.